Barbara Tavolari
Marilena Caciorgna

# SIENA
# Cathedral Baptistery

sillabe

ISBN 978-88-8347-407-1

Livorno
www.sillabe.it
info@sillabe.it

managing editor: *Maddalena Paola Winspeare*
lay-out: *Laura Belforte*
editing: *Giulia Bastianelli*
translation: *Catherine Burnett*

photolithography: *La Nuova Lito-Firenze*

photo credits: *Archivio Opera della Metropolitana;
Archivio Sillabe: Foto C. Cascioli, A. Quattrone; Foto Lensini, Siena*

printed by *Media Print, Livorno*

Reprint                              Year
2 3 4 5 6 7 8 9 10      2013 2014 2015 2016 2017 2018 2019 2020

This guide, written by Barbara Tavolari, aims to let visitors discover and appreciate Siena's most important church, its historical, religious and civil significance and its role as an open museum whose works of art have remained in their original positions over time.

The Cathedral is an extremely interesting place which is in many ways unique and conserves treasures of inestimable artistic and architectural value. The façade was first constructed under the supervision of Giovanni Pisano and is thought to have been completed, from a structural point of view, by Camaino di Crescentino. Its reliefs, niches, pinnacles and columns make the Cathedral one of the most important monuments of Siena's most artistically and culturally creative era.

As a symbol of the community's spiritual nature the Cathedral is characterised by the extraordinary magnificence of the exterior and more especially by the superb and evocative decoration of the interior. The Cathedral's construction and decoration was long and laborious. Over the centuries some of the greatest masters of all time worked for the Opera della Metropolitana and bestowed countless masterpieces on this venerated temple. Some of the most well-known artists include Nicola and Giovanni Pisano, Duccio di Buoninsegna, Antonio Federighi, Donatello, Pinturicchio, Domenico Beccafumi, Michelangelo and Bernini.

A small part of the guide is about the Crypt which was rediscovered after being hidden under heaps of debris for over seven centuries and is now on public display in all its radiant glory.

The Cathedral is an everlasting museum whose rich heritage is supported by this new guidebook. Through the publication of

carefully selected information it can, I hope, provide visitors with a effective means of fully understanding the changes which have marked our great Cathedral's transformation.

The Parish Church of San Giovanni, or rather the Sienese Baptistery, is one of the countless masterpieces of the Opera della Metropolitana's rich patrimony. This section of the guide was written by Marilena Caciorgna.

The architecture originates from the medieval era as construction work started well before the official decision to enlarge the Cathedral was made on the 23rd August 1339. The expansion project included a new transept extending into the Vallepiatta area of Siena but the work was never completed. This was because of both the statics problems linked to the construction of the cathedral and the terrible plague of 1348.

The Baptistery of Siena, however, is mentioned in every history of art manual because it contains at least one extraordinary work. The Baptismal Font has been described by historians as a kind of "anthology" of the foremost sculptors of the Tuscan Renaissance as it was worked on by Jacopo della Quercia, Lorenzo Ghiberti and even Donatello. This great Florentine artist had a steady relationship with the Sienese Opera della Metropolitana and made the gilded bronze relief of Herod's Banquet, the two statues of Faith and Hope, two musical angels (a third can be found in Berlin at the Staatliche Museen, Skulpturensammlung) and he may have conceived the design for a statue of Fortitude. We are not able to admire Donatello's Madonna and Child on the door of the shrine as it was surprisingly and regrettably refused by the Opera, who preferred Giovanni di Turino's design.

The Parish Church of San Giovanni holds the largest religious cycle of the Sienese Renaissance (the magnificent cycle which decorates the Pellegrinaio of Santa Maria della Scala actually has a profane quality). The series I am referring to is the succession of frescoes on the vaulting by Lorenzo di Pietro, known as 'Vecchietta'. This is a depiction of the Apostles and the Articles of the Creed, a quite original and profoundly theological theme which was particularly present in Siena from the medieval era onwards. The Articles of the Baptistery are about the Apostolic Symbol with which the Fathers of the Church designated the rule or profession of faith required to become baptised. Its portrayal is therefore particularly well-suited to this sacred place.

Considering the presence of this, and other less well-known treasures, I am delighted to be able to present this guide which takes into account the most recent critical studies. It helps visitors to discover the Sienese Cathedral and Baptistery and leaves them with a pleasant memento of two of the most significant monuments of Italian and European art.

Mario Lorenzoni

*Rector, Opera della Metropolitana, Siena*

# Cathedral

*Barbara Tavolari*

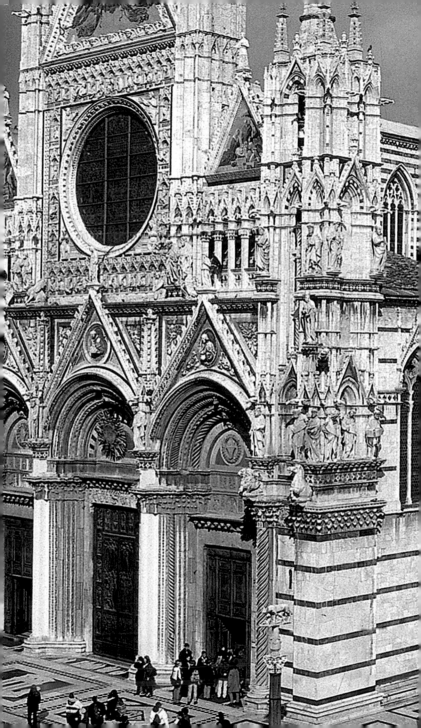

# Origins

The Cathedral of Siena is dedicated to Our Lady of the Assumption and sits in a central position at the top of a long flight of steps in a square of the same name. The extraordinary façade in polychrome marble along with the white and green strata on the side sum up and effectively demonstrate the linear and chromatic style of the Sienese Gothic era in a most complex and significant way.

The historical and structural events surrounding the construction of the Siense Cathedral recorded by critiques are not precise or reliable, especially between the ninth and eleventh centuries. It is presumed that in the tenth century there was already a cathedral of modest dimensions dedicated to St. Mary (Santa Maria) in the area where the Cathedral stands today. It actually stood at right angles to the new construction and had a parsonage and a bishop's residence annexed to it.

According to quite reliable sources the new cathedral with the façade facing the Hospital of Santa Maria della Scala was consecrated by Pope Alexander III Bandinelli on the 18th November 1179.

A valuable document from 1215 written by the cleric Odericus (*Ordo officiorum Senensis Ecclesiae*) provides important information about the church. On this date the construction work appeared to be in full swing and the building almost finished. From 1226 onwards payments for the marble facings on the building and the bell tower are recorded and they are documented as being finished in 1264. The bell tower is clearly in the roman style as demonstrated by its square design and octagonal steeple surrounded by four little pyramid-shaped steeples. On each side there are six rows of windows ranging from the single-lancet window below to the sextuple-lancet window above. The dome was finished at around the same time. It was covered in lead and an "apple" or sphere of copper was placed at the top (1263). The external part of the tambour has a double row of porticoes with little acute arches on twin columns below and on a single small column above. While the external work proceeded the Opera della Metropolitana was adding precious furnishings inside including the extraordinary marble Pulpit sculpted between 1265 and 1269 by Nicola Pisano and his collaborators (Giovanni Pisano, Arnolfo di Cambio and Lapo). From 1317 onwards extension work on the Cathedral into the Vallepiatta area of Siena commenced. The work began under the supervision of the sculptor and architect Tino di Camaino. He became master mason in 1320 but he had been working in the Cathedral since 1315. He set about the task with alacrity at least until 1339 when plans for the New Cathedral were officially approved (23rd August 1339).

This ambitious undertaking included the construction of a new longitudinal building which was to house the transept of the new cathedral. It was meant to extend at a 90 degree angle from the existing building into the current Piazza

Jacopo della Quercia. The construction work on the new and imposing ecclesiastical building was
overseen by the master mason Giovanni d'Agostino and progressed
at a good pace until the terrible
plague of 1348. Aside from the
plague, which caused an abrupt
interruption to proceedings, seri-
ous structural and statics errors
forced the Consiglio dell'Opera to
halt the construction work. All that
remains of this ambitious project
is the staggering façade, known as
the "Facciatone" (great façade) by
the Sienese people, and the right-
hand nave. The nave's first three
bays have been closed in and now
hold the Museo dell'Opera. The
splendid door which opened onto the right-hand side of the new

Cathedral also remains. Its spiral
columns and finely carved pillars
perfectly reflect the preference for
gothic elegance and stylised ornamentation typical of fourteenth
century Siena. The renowned
sculptural grouping of *Blessing
Christ between two angels* by Giovanni d'Agostino can also be seen
there. From the 1350s onwards
when the New Cathedral had
been abandoned, work on Baptistery's façade and the expansion
of the Cathedral's choir started
up again (after the suspension of
the construction work in 1339, as
mentioned above). The expansion
work meant that the ancient main
altar with the *Maestà* by Duccio
had to be moved and the apsidal
circular window frame with the

stained glass window by the same artist had to be repositioned. The work came to an end around the middle of the 1360s and from that moment onwards the artists' and the Opera del Duomo's attention was centred on the internal fittings with very few developments made on a structural level.

*"Facciatone"*

*View of the Bell Tower and the New Cathedral*

*Gateway of the New Cathedral*

# Façade

The façade can be divided into two sections: the lower section with the gateways and the upper section with the large circular central window. Each section is subdivided into three parts and crowned by three triangles. On the lower section the pediments bear the busts of Sienese blessed men sculpted by Tommaso Redi in the seventeenth century: *Blessed Giovanni Colombini*, *Blessed Ambrogio Sansedoni* and *Blessed Andrea Gallerani*. Mosaics made by Venetian masters around the end of the nineteenth century can be seen on the upper section. The preparatory cartoons for these mosaics were done in 1878 by the Sienese painters Luigi Mussini and Alessandro Franchi. Mussini prepared the design for the central and right-hand pediments which depict the *Coronation of the Virgin* and the *Nativity*, while Franchi prepared the drawing for the left-hand web which depicts the *Presentation of Mary at the Temple*. Two corner towers stand on either side of the façade while

two other smaller towers can be seen on the upper section either side of the large circular window. These towers help to draw in the perspective but their height is cut short by the strong horizontality of the three large, embrasured gateways in the lower section. The façade's lack of uniformity probably stems from the fact that it was constructed over a long period of time. The work went on for over thirty years and was overseen by more than one master mason.

In May 1284 the bishop of Siena, Rinaldo Malavolti, blessed the first stone of the new façade. Between 1285 and 1297 the Cathedral's designer Giovanni Pisano worked solely on the lower section. Towards the end of the century strong differences of opinion arose between Pisano and the Opera culminating in the artist's sudden departure from Siena before the façade was finished. Camaino di Crescentino was named as master mason in 1299 and

*Alessandro Franchi,* Presentation of Mary at the Temple, *Museo dell'Opera*

*Luigi Mussini,* Coronation of the Virgin, *Museo dell'Opera*

found he had to reorganise the worksite and replace almost the entire workforce. Building work proceeded at a good pace even though there was a brief pause in 1317 when the patrons gave the order to concentrate solely on the Cathedral's expansion to the east with the construction of the new choir and the Baptistery.

Work on the façade did not continue until the second half of the fourteenth century (1376) under the management of Giovanni di Cecco. The new project for the façade's completion was considerably different to Pisano's original design and was clearly inspired by the magnificent gothic façade of the Cathedral of Orvieto built by Lorenzo Maitani in the early fourteenth century. This is when the tricuspid crowning and the large circular window

As it has already been established, the phases of construction and the phases of sculptural decoration on the façade were interrupted. It is therefore important to look at the grandiose cycle designed by Giovanni Pisano in more detail. In actual fact, the way the sculptor arranged his multitude of statues on the façade is very precise. Architecturally speaking they take on a completely autonomous significance and cease to be simple decorative elements. Giovanni creates a tribute to the Virgin Mary and the Immaculate Conception which takes form through the insertion in the niches of ancient Greek philosophers, prophets from the Judaic and pagan worlds and Sibyls. In terms of style he firmly breaks with the Italian and French tradition to draw closer to classic antiquity. Besides these figures each niche has a cartouche with an inscription, presumably suggested by ecclesiastical scholars. Pisano also added some sculptures of animals as symbols of the religious journey including horses, lions, a winged calf and a griffon.

The statues' original positions have unfortunately not been maintained as arbitrary rearrangements and substitutions took place when the architect Giuseppe Partini was asked to redo the façade's upper middle section (1866-1869). Afterwards the original statues were substituted in part by copies by the sculptors Arnaldo Prunai, Fulvio Corsini and Umberto Cambi. During the

flanked by pillars with steeples appeared. The circular window is surrounded by thirty-six niches containing busts of patriarchs and the *Madonna and Child* can be seen in the centre (these are copies, the originals are kept in the Museo dell'Opera). On either side of the window there are two small loggia with five acute trefoil arches and an openwork transenna used as vantage point.

Second World War the façade underwent further changes and began to resemble its original form even less. Then at the beginning of the 1960s all the original statues were moved into the Museo dell'Opera.

The beautiful architrave on the central gateway which completes this great marble venture must not be forgotten. It was originally thought to be by Tino di Camaino but modern critiques consider it to be by Giovanni Pisano. The *Stories of Joachim, Anne and the Virgin* are depicted there and anticipate the style of the prophets which Pisano later sculpted with violent pathos.

Two magnificent columns stand next to the gateway. These were removed in 1967 along with the two lions above and substituted with copies in 1998 (the originals are on display in the Museo dell'Opera).

The acanthus ornamentation covered with various putti and animals is evidence of Giovanni Pisano's rich artistic culture. He reworked motifs from the classical tradition which could be seen in the Middle Ages on pillars from the Severan era in the Oratory of Pope John VII in the old St. Peter's Basilica. This type of ornamentation was also seen on roman architecture in Tuscany, for example on the east gateway of the Baptistery of Pisa and on the central gateways of the cathedrals in Pisa and Lucca, although the luxuriance, polymorphism and profundity of the Sienese stems and figures are very different from the less deeply incised designs in Pisa and Lucca. The Sienese sculpting shows immense supple energy reminiscent of the ornamentation on pulpits by Giovanni and it almost entirely covers the central gateway's columns. More than six centuries later, in the year 1958, the

*Giovanni Pisano,* Columns, *Museo dell'Opera*

sculptor Enrico Manfrini forged a bronze door with scenes of the *Glorification of the Virgin* for the same gateway. It must be said, however, that in 1457 the Sienese government held Donatello in high esteem and tried to induce him to stay in the city and live there until the end of his days working on the cathedral. One of the most important tasks offered to the sculptor was the making of two large bronze antae for the Cathedral's central gateway. Donatello worked on these antae between the end of 1457 and spring of 1458 but the fusion was never completed and the artist left the town soon after without any intention of going back again.

*Giovanni Pisano*, Lions, *Museo dell'Opera*

# Interior

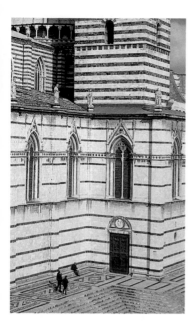

*Door of 'Forgiveness'*

*Donatello*, Madonna del Perdono,
*Museo dell'Opera*

The Cathedral had four entrances: the façade's three main gateways and the door on the right-hand side at the foot of the bell tower. This entrance is known as the Door of 'Forgiveness' ('Perdono') and was made by Francesco Mazzuoli in 1677 after the demolition of the archbishop's residence close by (1658). There is a copy of a roundel by Donatello in the lunette with the *Madonna del Perdono (Forgiving Virgin)*. It was once on the old altar of the Madonna of the Graces and is now in the Museo dell'Opera's collection. The bronze doorknockers are decorated with four panels featuring *Dedications to Mary of the town*, a modern work by the sculptor Vito Consorti (1946).

The interior is in the form of a Latin cross and has twenty-six pillars in various styles decorated with alternate layers of black and white marble. The same marble finishing was used on the walls of the temple to create a chromatic and perspectival effect which enthrals and amazes whoever enters the Cathedral. The magnificent capitals on the columns are decorated with phytomorphic motifs and some of them are thought to have been sculpted by Nicola Pisano as he worked on the Cathedral's pulpit in the 1260s. The vaults are painted in blue and scattered with gold stars. Their frames are decorated with candelabras interspersed with clypei with golden rosettes and the coats of arms of Siena.

*Central nave capital*                    *Counterfaçade*

*Central nave cross vault*

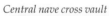

Two large marble columns rise up on the counterfaçade on either side of the central gateway. They are extraordinarily well-sculpted with acanthus racemes, eagles, putti and gargoyles and according to the inscription on the bottom of the right-hand column they were made in 1483 by Giovanni di Stefano. The columns actually came from the remains of the Four Crowned Saints altar (the first in the left-hand nave) which Giovanni worked on from 1473 onwards, clearly drawing inspiration from the columns sculpted by Pisano for the façade's central gateway two centuries previously. The bases of the columns feature *Stories of the Virgin* and were sculpted in bas-relief by Urbano da Cortona. They came from the demolished chapel of the Madonna of the

*Urbano da Cortona,* Parting from St. John, *counterfaçade*

*Giovanni di Meuccio di Contadino,* Stories of St. Ansanus, *counterfaçade*

Graces which once stood in the Cathedral's right-hand nave.

The architrave supported by the columns holds a frieze with four bas-reliefs depicting *Stories of St. Ansanus* by Giovanni di Meuccio di Contadino. These were originally in the old chapel of St. Ansanus (fifteenth century). On the walls of the loggia over the gateway there are four other bas-reliefs by Urbano di Cortona. These also came from the chapel of the Madonna of the Graces and depict *Stories of the Virgin*.

Right against the two entrance pillars there are two magnificent holy-water stoups sculpted between 1465 and 1467 by Antonio Federighi. The first stoup to be completed was the one on the left. Its basin is propped up by eagles tearing at serpents with their claws while some putti on the shaft sit on graceful dolphins. In contrast the stoup on the right has more imaginative and visionary ornamentation. A series of little dragons hanging by their tails from the higher part of the basin are able to bite the turtles which support the structure while some male nudes with their hands tied behind their backs are depicted on the shaft.

The central nave has a cornice which runs high up along the whole length of the church until it reaches the apse. It is decorated with the heads of pontiffs from Giovanni di Stefano's workshop which were made with terracotta moulds. These were made by the master furnacemen the Mazzaburroni brothers from 1495 on-

wards. Once they were painted the heads were quite monotonous and repetitive because only four or five moulds were used. Underneath, between the corner clypei on each arch, there is a series of thirty-six busts of roman emperors from Constantine to Theodosius. Statues of the *Apostles* by Giovanni Pisano originally stood next to the pillars in the central nave but these were substituted in the middle of the seventeenth century with statues of the same subject by Giuseppe Mazzuoli. Pisano's statues were repositioned along the cornices of the external pillars on the right-hand

*Antonio Federighi,* Holy-water stoup, *left pillar*

*Antonio Federighi,* Holy-water stoup, *right pillar*

*Heads of Popes, cornice*

side of the Cathedral and during the last quarter of the nineteenth century they were put in the Museo dell'Opera and replaced with copies. Mazzuoli's Apostles, on the other hand, were bought by English Catholics in 1871 and placed in the Brompton Oratory in London were they can still be seen today.

The hexagonal dome becomes a dodecahedron higher up and is supported by six pillars. In the pillars' pendentives there are six large statues in gilded stucco made around 1488 by Giovanni di Stefano depicting the *Patron Saints of the Town, St. Catherine* and *St. Bernardine*. In the running balcony there are forty-two monochrome painted figures of *Prophets* and *Patriarchs* made in 1481 by Guidoccio Cozzarelli and Benvenuto di Giovanni. The external part of the vault was completely renovated in 1664 and is covered with gilded panels decorated with stars which decrease in number towards the small dome. Right against the dome's first two pillars there are two very long poles. As tradition has it these poles were from the Florentine army's *carroccio* (war chariot) which was captured at Montaperti by the Sienese in 1260.

In the presbytery area of the cathedral there are two beautiful organs. The one on the top left, above the door which leads to the Sacristy, was made by Antonio Barili and his nephew Giovanni and completed in 1535. The one on the right-hand wall, based on a design by Riccio, was carved by Domenico di Maestro Lorenzo, an organ-maker from Lucca.

On either side of the bell tower door there are six bas-reliefs with *Stories of the Virgin* which Urbano da Cortona made for the Chapel of the Madonna of the Graces in the second half of the fifteenth century. The funerary monument of Bishop Piccolomini del Testa can be seen just above the door.

*Nineteenth-century photograph of the inside of the Cathedral with the statues by Mazzuoli*

# Paintings

## ■ Paintings on the Altars

The polychrome marble altars with their imposing columns are dominated by tympana on the interior walls. They are all fifth- and sixth-century reconstructions of older altars which were in the Cathedral, enhanced by resplendent paintings on wood with gold backgrounds by the most prominent Sienese artists of the time such as Duccio di Buoninsegna, Simone Martini, Pietro and Ambrogio Lorenzetti and Sassetta and Matteo di Giovanni. Many of these paintings were removed from the altars and lost, if not sold like the magnificent third century panel with a gold background by Simone Martini depicting the *Annunciation*. This panel was made for the St. Ansanus altar and is currently in the Uffizi Gallery in Florence. Most of the panels which remained in Siena are now kept in the Museo dell'Opera. These include Duccio's *Maestà* which was formerly on the main altar, the famous *Nativity of the Virgin* by Pietro Lorenzetti (1342), the *Madonna of Humility and Saints* by Gregorio di Cecco (1423) and the *Enthroned*

*Pietro Lorenzetti,* Nativity of the Virgin, *Museo dell'Opera*

*Matteo di Giovanni,* Enthroned Madonna with St. John the Evangelist, St. Nicolas, St. Gregory and St. Jerome, *Museo dell'Opera*

*Duccio di Buoninsegna,* Maestà *, Museo dell'Opera*

*Raffaello Vanni*, Ecstasy of St. Francis de Sales, *right nave, third altar*

---

*Madonna with St. John the Evangelist, St. Nicolas, St. Gregory and St. Jerome* by Matteo di Giovanni (1480).

The first altar proceeding along the right-hand nave is dedicated to St. Cajetan and holds a painting by the Bolognese artist Domenico Maria Canuti, a pupil of Guido Reni. It depicts the *Assumption of the Madonna with St. Cajetan of Thiene* (1681). The next altar is the Celsi altar with a seventeenth-century painting by Annibale Mazzuoli depicting the *Ecstasy of St. Jerome* (1725). The third altar is dedicated to St. Francis de Sales and holds a painting by Raffaello Vanni with the *Ecstasy of St. Francis de Sales* (1664). The painting is part of the artist's mature work and in spite of the evident experimentation with the Baroque style of Pietro da Cortona, the composition

is hardened by the use of sharp and severe lines. Until the middle of the seventeenth century the Chapel of the Madonna of the Graces sat in the place of this altar. It was built in the second half of the fifteenth century to hold the late thirteenth-century panel by Dietisalvi di Speme depicting the highly venerated *Madonna and Child*. This panel is now on the altar of the Chapel of the Madonna of the Vow (Chigi Chapel). During Alexander VII's papacy there was a fervent craze for rebuilding and renovation. The chapel was torn down and the remains of its marble blocks were either used in construction on other parts of the church or moved into the Museo dell'Opera.

The last altar of the right-hand nave is dedicated to St. Catherine and holds a painting by the Florentine artist Piero Dandini depicting the *Mystical Marriage of St. Catherine* (1678). The influence of Pietro da Cortona is highly evident in this painting.

The first altar proceeding along the right-hand transept was originally called the altar of the Crucifix but it is now dedicated to St. Crescentius. In 2006 an important discovery was made which changed its appearance. When restorers set about removing a painting on canvas by Luigi Mussini with the *Miracle of St. Crescentius* they discovered a fifteenth-century painting on wood underneath. The panel is attributed to the Master of the Osservanza and depicts two *Sorrowful Angels* which stand out against a starry blue sky. When this panel was removed for restoration a fresco attributed to Martino di Bartolomeo (1405) depicting the

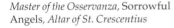

*Master of the Osservanza,* Sorrowful Angels, *Altar of St. Crescentius*

*Martino di Bartolomeo,* Sorrowful Angels, *Altar of St. Crescentius*

same subject was discovered but it is unfortunately in a terrible state. A wooden *Crucifix* originally hung behind the fresco and figures of the *Sorrowful* by Domenico di Niccolò were placed next to it in 1415. These are now in the Museo dell'Opera. Following the seventeenth-century renovations overseen by Dionisio Mazzuoli the wooden structure was substituted in 1651 with a painting by the Florentine artist Giovanni Maria Moranti depicting *St. Philip Neri* (1680). This was substituted in turn in 1869 with Luigi Mussini's painting of *St. Crescentius*.

The second altar along the right-hand nave is dedicated to St. Bernardine and holds a masterpiece of post-Caravaggian Italian art, a painting by Mattia Preti depicting the *Sermon of St. Bernardine.* The work was done by the artist in Malta around 1670 and he arrived in Siena a few years later (1675). Preti alternates penetrating shadows with bright light in order to make the figure of the preaching saint stand out from the scene. The influence of Caravaggio's style can be seen in this work but it has been revitalised by the artist's own experience in the studios of Venetian masters such as Paolo Veronese and Tintoretto.

The next monument is the Chapel of the Sacrament with the beautiful altar of St. Victor (constructed by Flaminio del Turco in 1585). This altar holds the magnificent and joyful painting by Alessandro Casolani depicting the *Adoration of the Shepherds* (1594). Under the window inside the chapel there are five fifteenth-century bas-reliefs

*Luigi Mussini,* St. Crescentius, *Altar of St. Crescentius*

*Mattia Preti,* Sermon of St. Bernardine, *Altar of St. Bernardine*

*Alessandro Casolani,* Adoration of the Shepherds, *Altar of St. Victor*

in marble featuring the *Evangelists and St. Paul* by Giovanni Turini and Giovanni di Franceco da Imola.

The altar of St. Ansanus in the left-hand transept sits in a chapel which is also dedicated to the saint and holds a painting with *St. Ansanus baptising the Sienese people*. The painting was done by Francesco Vanni between 1593 and 1596 and is characterised by a strong mannerist style and a marked chromatic bravura providing evidence of the artist's meeting with Federico Barocci in 1585.

The next altar is dedicated to St. Savinus and holds a painting on canvas which was started by the mediocre Venetian artist Salvatore Fontana and finished by Francesco Vanni's son Raffaello. The painting depicts the *Madonna in Glory with St. Peter and St. Paul*. The St. Savinus altar is followed by the altar of the Crucifix, so called because of the mid-fourteenth century Crucifix hanging above it. The crucifix is wrongly identified as being from Montaperti as people originally believed that it was brought to the Cathedral by the Sienese people as a victory trophy after the bloody battle against the Florentines at Montaperti (1260).

In the seventeenth century three stucco sculptures by the Sienese sculptor Giuseppe Mazzuoli were placed on the altar next to the crucifix. They depict *Our Lady of Sorrows*, *St. John* and *Mary Magdalene*.

Straight after the Piccolomini altar along the left-hand nave, the altar of the Magi can be seen with an altarpiece depicting the *Epiphany* by the Sienese artist Pietro Sorri. Sorri was a late mannerist painter from the school of Salimbeni and Beccafumi who spent some time studying in Venice, so much so that this work displays a style of composition, a chromatic range and effects of light which are reminiscent of the work of Titian, Tintoretto and Veronese.

The last two altars along the nave hold paintings done by Francesco Trevisani around 1688. *Jesus with*

*Altar of the Four Crowned Saints*
*Bartolomeo Neroni known as Riccio,* Martyrdom of the Four Crowned Saints, *Museo dell'Opera*

*St. James and St. Philip* is on the altar of the Congregation of St. Peter while the first altar next to the entrance is dedicated to the Four Crowned Saints and holds the *Martyrdom of the Four Crowned Saints*. This thirteenth-century altar was destroyed at the end of the seventeenth century following the renovation work organised by Cardinal Flavio Chigi. It

originally held a magnificent fresco by Bartolomeo Neroni known as Riccio (1534-1535) but unfortunately the work was almost lost and only three sections are conserved in the Museo dell'Opera.

■ **Frescoes in the Apse**

Domenico Beccafumi was asked to decorate the apse in 1535, perhaps thanks to a recommendation by Baldassare Peruzzi who had always admired his work and was also the designer of the new main altar and the large apsidal niche. To begin with Beccafumi frescoed the conch with the *Glory of Angels* which he completed around 1540. The work is characterised by a bustling multitude of figures and has a rayed triangle in the centre. This symbol of the Trinity was put there in 1812 by Francesco Mazzuoli in place of an image of the *Ascension* but unfortunately the

work was ruined by an earthquake in 1798. Underneath there is a painting of *Our Lady of the Assumption* by the Bolognese artist Bartolomeo Cesi (1594). It was originally meant for the Church of Certosa di Maggiano but it was put in the Cathedral in place of a fresco of the *Madonna with St. Peter and St. John* by Beccafumi. This painting was also seriously damaged during the earthquake.

The artist finished decorating the apse in 1544 when he painted four sections, two with *Angels* and two with *Apostles*. Following a personal interpretation of Michelangelo's style, the figures are characterised by a powerful monumentality, exalted by chromatic effects and chiaroscuro.

The stucco decoration which enriches the apse was also done by Beccafumi. He was able to unite the painted areas with an ornamental

*Domenico Beccafumi*, Glory of Angels, *apsidal conch*

ensemble of foliage and vegetal and candelabra shoots while two beautiful *Winged Victories* seem to fly gracefully above the apsidal niche as they hold up palms and olive wreaths.

The decorative work on the presbytery was not completed until 1608 when Ventura Salimbeni was asked to do four large frescoes. The artist started work on the frescoes two years later and the first panel with *Falling Manna* (left) carries a date and signature in the lower left corner (Ventura Salimbeni Sen. 1610). The artist completed *Esther and Ahasuerus* in the pendant (right) a year later then went on to do the lateral frescoes which depict *Sienese Saints and Blessed Men*. The composition is quite chaotic on the whole, crowded with a multitude of pompous figures but its best aspect is revealed in the little scenes in the background as they are full of interesting detail.

*Bartolomeo Cesi,* Our Lady of the Assumption, *apse*

*Ventura Salimbeni,* Sienese Saints and Blessed Men, *apsidal area*

# Sculptures

# ■ Pulpit

Siena Cathedral's Pulpit was sculpted by Nicola Pisano between 1265 and 1268 and epitomises one of the most outstanding phases in Italian sculptural art history. The artist had already sculpted the Pulpit for the Baptistery of Pisa a few years earlier (1260) but in Siena he really succeeded in creating an absolutely magnificent work of art. In comparison with the one in Pisa the Sienese monument reveals the artist's fully matured style. Nicola overcame the Romanic tradition to develop a style marked by classicism which cannot be considered a simple imitation, although it was a useful means of creating a more naturalistic depiction of landscape and the human form.

The Pulpit was originally near the main altar which was, at that time, under the dome. It was first restored in 1329 when the pure white Carrara marble columns which supported the pulpit were substituted with granite ones from ancient excavations in the town of Cosa. In 1543 the Pulpit was completed dismantled, put back together again in its current position and enhanced by a marble base for the nine columns and a large circular stairway made from a design by Bartolomeo Neroni known as Riccio. The octagonal pulpit is supported by eight columns positioned around its edge and one central column with depictions of the *Liberal Arts* on the base. The external columns rest alternately on the base and on the backs of lions or lionesses and they are connected by a series of little trefoil arches which sustain the actual pulpit. The arches are

*Nicola Pisano,* Pulpit
*Nicola Pisano,* Visitation, Nativity *(I scene)*

*Nicola Pisano*, Journey and Adoration of the Magi *(II scene)*

*Nicola Pisano*, Presentation at the Temple and Flight to Egypt *(III scene)*

*Nicola Pisano*, Slaughter of the Innocents *(IV scene)*

*Nicola Pisano*, Crucifixion *(V scene)*

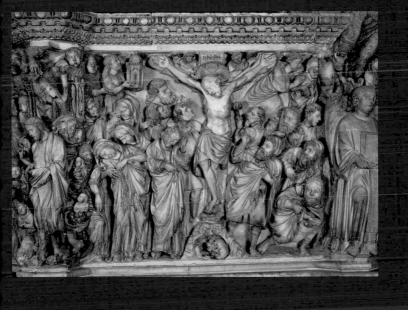

*Nicola Pisano*, Universal Judgement - the Elect *(VI scene)*

*Nicola Pisano*, Universal Judgement - the Reprobates *(VII scene)*

*Nicola Pisano*, Journey and Adoration of the Magi, *detail*

separated by little corner statues of the *Virtues* (Temperance, Humility, Hope, Fortitude, Faith, Charity, Prudence) while figures of *Prophets* and *Evangelists* are sculpted in the pendentives. The divine project for salvation is fully expressed in the stories on the seven panels in bas-relief which make up the balcony's parapet. The stories are divided by little corner pillars with allegorical statues depicting *Visitation and Nativity, Journey and Adoration of the Magi, Presentation at the Temple and Flight into Egypt, The Slaughter of the Innocents, Crucifixion and Universal Judgement* (over the last two panels). Nicola concentrates on the expressive power of movement, and the way the figures seem to come to life as they emerge from the surface heightens the dramatic force of the stories. The first scene of the *Nativity* is extraordinary, the large figure of the Madonna in the centre almost seems like a roman matron and the *Journey of the Magi* picture with the beautiful foreshortened portrayal of the horses and their graceful manes is full of character. In contrast, the Crucifixion scene is bursting with great dramatic force. The body of Christ acts as a caesura between the two groups of figures on either side thus creating two divergent lines which intensify the dramatic effect of the story. Furthermore, the highly characterised features reveal the artist's in depth study of the infinite expressive capability of the human body.

*Tino di Camaino,*
Monument of Cardinal
Petroni

*Neroccio Di Bartolomeo,*
Funerary Monument
of Bishop Tommaso
Piccolomini del Testa

## ■ Funerary Monuments

The sepulchral monument of Cardinal Petroni, who died in Genova in February 1314 and whose body was transported to Siena in March of the same year, was made in 1315 by Tino di Camaino, an artist who trained in Giovanni Pisano's workshop. This masterpiece of fourteenth-century sculpture was originally positioned where the Chapel of St. John currently stands. Alberto Aringhieri set up the monument in 1482 in the place of the Petroni family altar, dedicated to St. Catherine of the Wheel. It was initially positioned against the Chapel's left-hand wall then moved higher up in 1726 to make room for Zondadari's monumental baroque tomb but the lower part with the console and four caryatids was damaged. It was only restored to its original form in 1951 by Enzo Carli who had it moved to its current position in the Chapel of St. Ansanus. The sarcophagus is supported by the caryatids and holds three scenes sculpted in high relief with the life of Christ *post mortem*. Above, the cardinal lies on a chest unveiled by angels opening the curtains. At the top a niche with three cuspidal arches holds the statues of the *Madonna and Child* between *St. Peter* and *St. Paul*.

This work by Tino di Camaino seems to adhere to gothic forms reminiscent of Simone Martini and reflects the artist's meeting with the influx of French sculptors at the Neapolitan court of Robert d'Anjou. The sinuosity of line and smooth finish reveal Tino di Camaino's own style.

Inside the wall above the bell tower's little door visitors can find the sepulchral monument of Tommaso Piccolomini del Testa, who was appointed Bishop of Pienza by Pope Pius II in 1470. It was made by Neroccio Di Bartolomeo in 1485 and fully reflects the taste for cultural renewal of the second half of the fifteenth century dem-

onstrated by the grotesque ornamentation along the side pillars and on the frieze with vases, floral festoons, racemes and candelabras. The coffin is also in an antiquated style following the stylistic features of Renaissance art with a simulacrum lying in front of three red marble recessed panels. The whole monument is supported by two spiral brackets and two putti sculpted in the round rise above it. The putti hold the Piccolimini coat of arms which is crowned by a bishop's mitre.

The tombstone of Tommaso Pecci, Bishop of Grossetto, lies in the paving of the left transept inside the confines of the Chapel

*Donatello,* Tombstone of Bishop Pecci

of St. Ansanus. It was commissioned from Donatello in 1427 as there is a signature and date on the inside of the cartouche being unrolled by two putti at the dead man's feet. The cartouche also contains two shields with the Pecci family coat of arms. These were once coloured but now only a few traces can be seen. The figure of the bishop, in bas-relief, is portrayed with his hands folded together across his chest, the mitre and the pastoral staff. The curl of the pastoral staff is positioned almost sideways giving the work depth, just like the foreshortened feet with visible soles. The aspiration for realism pursued by Donatello and the desire to create an illusion of three dimensionality make this work a revolutionary *unicum* in the iconographic spectrum of underground tombs. The creation of this bronze sculpture must have occupied Donatello for longer than he had anticipated as the slab was not sent to Siena from Padova until 1449–1452 (in three parts to make transportation easier). It was initially placed in the choir of the Cathedral where the bishop was buried then it was moved during the sixteenth century to its current position in the Chapel of St. Ansanus.

## ■ Main Altar

The main altar was originally under the dome surrounded by an ancient wooden choir. In 1317, when the extension work began on the Cathedral towards the Vallepiatta area of Siena, the altar was moved. It was repositioned for the second time in 1506 and then again in 1536 to the place where it stands today. The altar was reconstructed ex novo from a design by Baldassarre Peruzzi (1536) and is clearly marked by a roman style with its marble rectangles and squares arranged on top of one another and bordered by elegant framework. The magnificent bronze ciborium made by Lorenzo di Pietro known as Vecchietta between 1467 and 1471 is on the altar. The ciborium was originally in the church of the Spedale di Santa Maria della Scala (Hospital) and was transferred to the Cathedral in 1506 at the request of Pandolfo Petrucci, Lord of Siena. Due to its extraordinarily high quality the work took the place of the magnificent *Maestà* by Duccio di Buoninsegna (1308–1311) as Duccio's work was no longer representative of the fully developed Renaissance style.

Vecchietta's ciborium displays a refined approach, fully following the classic style of the second half of the fifteenth century. The base of the trunk is elegant and original, decorated with peacock feathers and make-believe animals which are reminiscent of those sculpted by Federighi for the holy-water stoups.

The body, held up by four angels, is characterised by a series of grates in knotted cord separated by niches with the *Theological Virtues* (Faith, Hope and Charity). Along the trabeation of the dome above the volutes there are four little winged angels with symbols of the passion in their hands. On the crowning of the actual dome a pair of angels hold up a chalice, a symbol of Faith, with the *Christ resurrected* above. The whole composition is brought to life by twenty-four figures in the round in various sizes and is one of Vechietta's best sculptural creations. In actual fact, the artist was able to reach an extraordinary

*Lorenzo di Pietro known as Vecchietta,*
Ciborium

Theological Virtues, *detail of the*
*Ciborium*

level of skill in bronze fusion with this work. It has a warm reddish tone which came to light after it was restored in 2006, returning the work to its original splendour. On either side of the magnificent ciborium there are two bronze *Angel candelabra holders* made by Giovanni di Stefano in 1490. This sophisticated sculptor was Sassetta's son and a pupil of Federighi. He forged the angels in the classical style recognizable by the clothes, the hairstyles, the gestures and the gentle faces. On the lower step there is another pair of graceful *Angels* made by Francesco di Giorgio Martini in 1490. Francesco's angelic figures were sculpted in bronze with captivating pictorial feeling and convey extraordinary lightness. They seem to hover without being weighed down over the marble base which is decorated with rosettes and acanthus swirls.

The altar's bronze ornamentation is completed by two little sprites on the side which are attributed to Domenico Beccafumi (1527–1536). During the following decade (1547–1551) the artist was busy making the eight *Angels* which adorn the columns rising up from the altar towards to the dome. These are splendid figures which seem to move with gentle grace. They have full, round faces where the bronze almost vibrates with a luminism reminiscent of the artist's pictorial work. The little consoles where the angels stand were also forged by Beccafumi and depict an original bearded man's head with leaves and fruit garlands.

*Giovanni di Stefano,* Angel candelabra holder

*Giovanni di Stefano,* Angel candelabra holder

*Francesco di Giorgio Martini,* Angel candelabra holder

*Francesco di Giorgio Martini,* Angel candelabra holder

### ■ Piccolomini Altar

In the early sixteenth century Michelangelo also came to work on the Cathedral. In 1501 Cardinal Francesco Piccolomini Todeschini asked Buonarroti to make fifteen statues for the Piccolomini altar in Siena Cathedral. The altar was conceived as a family tomb and sits against the wall of the Cathedral's left-hand nave near the Piccolomini Library. It was constructed by the Lombard sculptor Andrea Bregno between 1480 and 1485. It has a large central niche with an altar, an altarpiece and two pairs of niches on either side,

*Michelangelo,* St. Peter

*Michelangelo,* St. Paul

one above the other. In keeping with the common practice of the time to incorporate ancient painted panels in newer architectural structures, Cardinal Todeschini had a late fourteenth-century panel by Paolo di Giovanni Fei with the *Madonna of the Milk* (1390) inserted in the centre of the altar. The panel is now in the Museo dell'Opera. A niche below

a tympanum in the upper middle part of the altar holds the *Madonna and Child* by Giovanni di Cecco. On either side there are two bas-reliefs and two other niches. Unfortunately Michelangelo took on numerous tasks around this time and did not honour his contract. Between 1501 and 1504 he sent only four of the fifteen statues that had been commissioned to Siena from nearby Florence where he was working on the *David*. These included *St. Peter* and *St. Paul*, for the lower left and right niches respectively, *St. Augustine* (traditionally known as St. Pius) and *St. Gregory the Great*, for the upper left and right niches respectively. The *St. Paul* with his severe and concentrated expression is acknowledged to be the artist's first self-portrait and the *St. Peter* is characterised by a sculptural style reminiscent of classical art. The statues' plasticity and sense of movement as they turn express a heroic ideal typical of Michelangelo's maturity. In contrast, the *St. Augustine* and the *St. Gregory* don't display the same Michelangeloesque vigour but give way to a certain static quality and limited expressiveness. This commission probably plagued Michelangelo as he was so busy in Florence with important commissions like the *Doni Tondo*, the *Madonna of Bruges* and the abovementioned *David*, that he did not adjust well to working on Bregno's façade. Its severe linearity and composed fifteenth-century elegance enforced a number of intolerable restrictions on Buonarroti.

*Paolo di Giovanni Fei,* Madonna of the Milk, *Museo dell'Opera*

## ■ Statues of Pontiffs

During the second half of the seventeenth century, at the same time as construction work on the Chapel of the Vow went ahead, Alexander VII decided to proceed with another important decorative scheme for the Cathedral. In the late sixteenth century work had begun on a project to put in statues of Pope *Paul V Borghese* and *Pope Marcellus II Cervini* on the counterfaçade. The Chigi family's idea was to decorate the walls of the Cathedral with statues of all the Popes of Sienese origin. Hence the presence in the right-hand transept of a statue of *Alexander III*, an exquisite sculpture in a clear baroque style with a slightly asymmetric structure. The statue was started by the creative artist Melchiorre Caffà and completed by Ercole Ferrata in 1668. There is a monument to Alexander VII in front of it which was sculpted by Antonio Raggi in 1663 from a design by Gian Lorenzo Bernini. The figure is characterised by great solemnity and the broad motion of the arm in the act of blessing bestows the pontiff with a new vital force. In actual fact, Raggi was able to revitalise a sculptural style in this work which had hitherto characterised the statues of pontiffs. The cycle continues in the left-hand transept with the rather feeble statues of *Pius II Piccolomini* and *Pius III Piccolomini Todeschini*. These two sculptures were made in the late seventeenth century by the Sienese sculptors Giuseppe Mazzuoli

and Pietro Balestra respectively. These sculptors were also busy in Rome with Bernini working on Alexander VII's funerary monument in St. Peter's Basilica.

*Melchiorre Caffà and Ercole Ferrata,* Monument to Alexander III

*Giuseppe Mazzuoli,* Monument to Pius II

# Chapel of the
# Madonna of the Vo·v

*Dietisalvi di Speme,* Madonna of the Vow

*Gian Lorenzo Bernini,* Mary Magdalene

*Gian Lorenzo Bernini,* St. Jerome

The Chapel was constructed at the request of the Sienese pope Alexander VII by the Chigi family. They entrusted the task to the genius of the great baroque artist Gian Lorenzo Bernini. Construction work started 1658 and was overseen by the Sienese architect Benedetto Giovannelli. Giovannelli had previously been asked to take steps to renovate the Chapel of the Madonna of the Graces by the rector Ludovico de' Vecchi. Alexander VII immediately decided to take responsibility for the task upon himself and named the new chapel after his family. The buyer wanted to erect a structure which could hold the late thirteenth-century painting on wood which was a fragment of a larger composition by Dietisalvi di Speme of the *Madonna of the Vow*, venerated by the

Sienese people as the protectress of the town. In order to house the sacred image Bernini made an extraordinary gilded bronze frame held up by two angels with three other little angels at the top flying playfully in the lapis lazuli blue background.

The circular chapel has a gilded dome with hexagonal lacunars and a lantern decorated with cherubs. It is supported by eight magnificent columns in verd-antique marble from the Basilica of San Giovanni in Laterano in Rome. Four niches open out around the edge and contain marble sculptures. The first two near the entrance are *St. Jerome* and *Mary Magdalene* and they are signed by Bernini. They were made in Rome between 1661 and 1663 and sent to Siena in August of that year. The first statue is characterised by ascetic tension as the saint seems to be entranced by an ardent spiritual love for the crucifix he carries with devout ardour in his hands. The second statue is sculpted in a florid and sensual manner which expresses impassioned and languorous emotivity.

The two statues on either side of the altar are by Antonio Raggi (*St. Bernardine*) and Ercole Ferrata (*St. Catherine*), Bernini's two young collaborators who actually trained in the workshop of the classicist sculptor Alessandro Algardi.

Above the niches there are four marble bas-reliefs with *Stories of Mary* by Carlo Marchionni (*Birth of the Virgin*), Pietro Bracci (*Presentation of Mary at the Temple*), Filippo Valle (*Visitation of the Virgin*) and Battista Maini (*Death of the Virgin*).

On the left-hand wall there is a large painting by Carlo Maratta depicting the *Visitation* (1661–1664). The simple composition is pervaded by a great sense of serenity with the four imposing central characters adopting a relaxed, open stance. A gloria of winged putti and cherubs surround the scene. Maratta was from the Marches region of Italy and trained in Rome in Andrea Sacchi's workshop. His work was marked by classicist poetics but was not lacking in baroque influences. The picture on the right-hand wall depicting the *Flight into Egypt* was also originally by Maratta but it was substituted at the end of the eighteenth century (1793) with a mosaic of the same subject because its condition had deteriorated.

The bronze railing with oak racemes interspersed with little angels and stars is also magnificent. It was made by Giovanni Artusi in Rome in 1664.

The extraordinary and harmonious polychrome marble effect contributes to the chapel's magnificence. The colours vary from verd–antique to Siena yellow, red porphyry to Carrara white and the effect of the gold and lapis lazuli on the altar is especially resplendent.

# Chapel
# of St. John

The rector Alberto Aringhieri, a knight of the order of St. John, had this chapel built in 1486. It was intended to hold the reliquary of the arm of St. John which the despot of Morea, Tommaso Paleologo, had given to Pius II. In turn, the pontiff gave the reliquary to the Cathedral in 1464. In 1466 a silver urn with precious stones to hold the sacred remains was commissioned from the goldsmith Francesco d'Antonio. The urn is currently in the Museo dell'Opera. A chapel dedicated to St. Catherine used to stand in the place of the current chapel and the rector who preceded Aringhieri, Savino di Matteo (1467–1480), had wanted to build a chapel dedicated to the Sienese people's Baptist, St. Ansanus, in the same position. This is why two statues of the abovementioned saints appear in the lower niches on the sides. They were sculpted in 1487 by Giovanni di Stefano (*St. Ansanus*) and Neroccio di Bartolomeo (*St. Catherine*). One of Donatello's masterpieces sits in the central niche – a bronze sculpture of *St. John the Baptist*. The statue was made by the artist in Florence in 1457 but was not positioned in the chapel until 1501.

*Neroccio di Bartolomeo,* St. Catherine

*Giovanni di Stefano,* St. Ansanus

*Francesco d'Antonio,* Reliquary for the arm of St. John, *Museo dell'Opera*

*Donatello,* St. John the Baptist

The sculpture was cast in three parts and was missing a right arm. This was forged by Vecchietta in 1474 using a method which was certainly far removed from Donatello's technique. Unlike Vecchietta, who shaped the material with cold perfectionism, the Florentine master worked the surface as if he were stripping the flesh off a body in a fierce and agonising maceration of form. The figure of the Baptist is, in fact, rough and dramatic with its limbs racked with pain and its facial expression sunken with suffering.

The circular chapel's interior is based on a design by Francesco di Giorgio Martini. In the lower part there is a pink marble plinth which

*Pinturicchio,* Portrait of a knight

*Pinturicchio,* Portrait of Alberto Aringhieri

sits between white cornices. Above it there is a double row of panels which used to contain eight frescoes with *Stories of the Baptist,* commissioned in 1504 from Pinturicchio. Only five of these panels were in the artist's hand, the other three (*Visitation, Decollation of St. John, Baptism of Jesus*) were damaged by humidity and substituted at the beginning of the seventeenth century by Francesco Rustici (1608). In the second half of the nineteenth century (1866) the panel with the *Visitation* was redone once again by the artist Cesare Maccari who changed the iconographic subject to depict the *Imprisonment of St. John.*

In the centre of the chapel there is a small basin for holy water sculpted by Antonio Federighi (around 1460). It has an octagonal structure and the panels are separated by fluted columns. The scenes sculpted on the panels are *Creation of Adam, Creation of Eve, Eve tempted by the serpent, Eve offering the apple to Adam, God chastising Adam and Eve, Expulsion from Eden, Hercules and the lion* and *Hercules fighting the Centaur.* Graceful figures of putti, dragons and dolphins are portrayed on the fascia of the base and the frieze following a perfect classical style which would continue to develop and become more

RHODI

and more apparent in Federighi's mature work. The chapel's façade was done entirely in marble by the Sienese sculptor Giovanni di Stefano. Giovanni was joined in the task by one of his most promising pupils, Lorenzo di Mariano known as Marrina. Marrina was also involved in the construction of the Piccolomini Library a few years later.

The yellow marble columns at the entrance of the chapel stand on two beautiful bases. The right-hand one was sculpted by Antonio Federighi before the chapel was constructed and reflects the artist's mature style revealing classi-cal motifs like wreaths of flowers and fruit, goat heads and mytho-logical scenes such as Hercules and the Lion. The left-hand base is by Giovanni di Stefano and in order to keep the ensemble harmonious he decorated it with similar motifs to those on the base by Federighi.

All of the external ornamentation is marked by an ancient style: winged victories, putti, festoons and pilasters with military motifs. The military motifs are a clear reference to the person who commissioned the work as Alberto Aringhieri was a member of the Order of the Knights of St. John (which later became the Knights

of Malta), strenuous defenders of Christianity against the invasion of the Turks. Pinturicchio also paid homage to Aringhieri in one of the internal frescoes with a portrait which shows him at prayer wearing the black mantle with the white cross of the Order of the Knighthood.

On the left of Chapel's entrance a baroque monument of the knight Alessandro Zondadari stands against the wall. It was started in 1725 by Giuseppe Mazzuoli and completed by his nephew Bartolomeo.

*Antonio Federighi,* Basin for holy water

*Antonio Federighi,* Base of the column at the entrance, *right*

# Piccolomini
# Library

To honour the memory of his maternal uncle, Enea Silvio Piccolomini (Pope Pius II), and to look after the rich bibliographical heritage the pontiff and humanist collected when he was in Rome, Cardinal Francesco Todeschini Piccolomini, archbishop of Siena (later Pope Pius III), had a library built along the north-west side in the old canonical area of the Cathedral around 1492. Todeschini was inspired both by the French tradition which allowed libraries to be annexed to cathedrals and the opening of the Vatican Library

by Sixtus IV. The Vatican Library also encapsulated the renaissance objective of creating an institution which was both a centre for study and an artistic illustration of the "Modern Era".

The external marble façade was the down to the artistry of the Sienese sculptor-carver Lorenzo di Mariano known as Marrina. It has twin arches sustained by three pillars with finely decorated candelabras incorporating putti, amphorae and cornucopias decorated with figures and cornucopia which spread out under a frieze.

The frieze is richly decorated with objects in the ancient style such as griffins, eagles with open wings and floral vases. The double arch is closed by lunettes which carry the coats of arms of Cardinal Francesco (capped by a cardinal's hat) and Pius II (capped by a papal tiara). The coats of arms are held up by putti sculpted in the round and underneath there is another frieze decorated with putti on seahorses.

On the right of the entrance behind a double bronze railing by Antonio Ormanni known as Toniolo (1497), there is an altar with a bas-relief in the centre by Giovanni di Stefano depicting *St. John the Evangelist*. This was originally positioned on the crown of the Chapel of St. John. A wooden sculptural grouping with the *Pietà* by Alberto di Betto, which came from the altar of the Crucifix, used to be under the altar table but it was transferred to the Superintendency of Siena in 2006 to be restored before being placed in the Museo dell'Opera. The Library's façade is dominated by a large fresco depicting the Coronation of Pius III made by Pinturicchio in 1505. Inside the Library, above the entrance, Marrina placed a stucco high relief in a niche depicting the *Expulsion from Eden*. This was done in homage to Jacopo della Quercia, the great Sienese sculptor and creator of a panel with the same subject for the Gaia Fountain.

The walls are covered with brilliant frescoes made between 1505 and 1507 by the great Umbrian Master Bernardino di Betto, better known as Pinturicchio. The frescoes are divided into ten frames by faux candelabra pillars which stand on bases decorated with the Piccolomini coat of arms and are flanked by a pairs of putti. In turn, stories of the life of Pius II are depicted in faux arches which form a loggia. There is an inscription in Latin under each story which explains the events according to Pius II's biography by the Humanist writer Giovanni Antonio Campano.

The story of Pius II's life starts with the episode in the frame next to the large right-hand window at the end of the room. It proceeds in a chronological order along the walls until it

*Wooden benches containing illuminated choir books*

*Pinturicchio*, Departure for Basel of Enea Silvio Piccolomini

AENEAS·SILVIVS·PICOLOMINEVS·NATVS·EST·PATRE·SILVIO·MATRE·VI
CTORIA·XVIII·OCTOB·ANN·MCCCCV·CORSIANI·INFVNDI3
GENTILITIIS·BASILEAM·AD·CONCILIVM·CONTENDENS·VI·TEMPESTA
TIS·IN·LYBIAM·PROPELLITVR·

HIC AENEAS AFOELICE·V·ANTIPAPA LEGATVS AD FEDERICVM·III·
CAESAREM MISSVS LAVREA CORONA DONATVR ET INTER AMICOS
EIVS AC SECRETARIVS ANNVMERATVR ET PRAEFICITVR·

*Pinturicchio,* Frederick III crowns Enea Silvio Piccolomini a poet

reaches the large left-hand window. The scenes are as follows: *Departure for Basel of Enea Silvio Piccolomini; Oration of Enea Silvio Piccolomini before King James I of Scotland; Frederick III crowns Enea Silvio Piccolomini a poet; Subjugation of Enea Silvio Piccolomini to Pope Eugene IV; Enea*

*Pinturicchio,* Subjugation of Enea Silvio Piccolomini to Pope Eugene IV

*Silvio Piccolomini presents Eleanor of Aragon to Frederick III at the Camollia gate; Enea Silvio Piccolomini nominated Cardinal by Callisto III; Enea Silvio Piccolomini elected Pope under the name of Pius II, Pius II presides over the Congress of Mantua; Pius II canonises St. Catherine; Pius II reaches Ancona for the Crusade against the Turks.*

The episodes of Pius II's life are characterised by extraordinary creative and decorative geniality. The variety of brilliant and bright colours is never-ending and the luxurious rooms and clothes comprehensively embody the

PIVS CVM ANCON· EXPEDITIONE IN TVRCOS ACCELERARET EX
FEBRE INTERIIT CVIVS ANIMAM HEREMITA CAMALDVLEN· INCOE
LVM EFFERRI VIDIT CORPVS VERO PATRVM DECRETO INVRBEM
REPORTATVM EST·

*Pinturicchio,* Pius II reaches Ancona      Rape of Proserpine, *ceiling fresco*
for the Crusade against the Turks

refined renaissance culture. The scenes contain various gentle and graceful figures and take place against a background of idyllic landscapes with enchanting seascapes, buildings, churches and loggia with spectacular architecture and slender saplings against crystalline skies.

The vault's triangular webs are completely decorated with grotesques of mythological subjects. On the longer sides there are eight rectangular sections with scenes of satyrs, nymphs and tritons while the four sections on the shorter sides hold *Charity*, *Peace*, *Wisdom* and *Truth*, followed by two large panels with the *Rape of Proserpine* and *Diana and Endymion*. In the centre of the vault there is a large Piccolomini family coat of arms with golden moons on a blue background.

The marble sculptural group the *Three Graces* sits in the centre of the room. It is a roman copy of a Hellenistic pictorial design which was bought in Rome by Cardinal Todeschini and transported to Siena

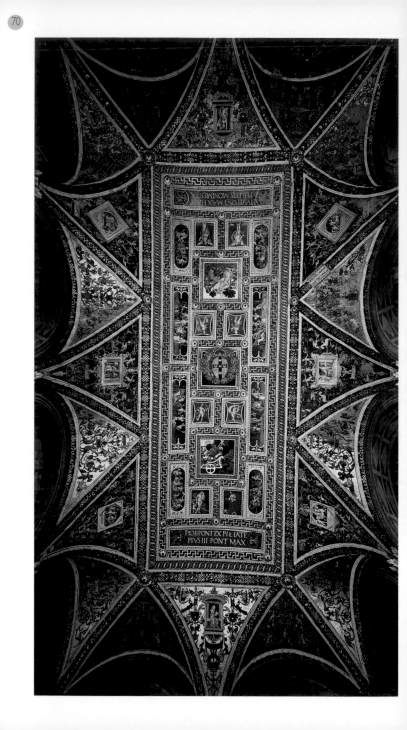

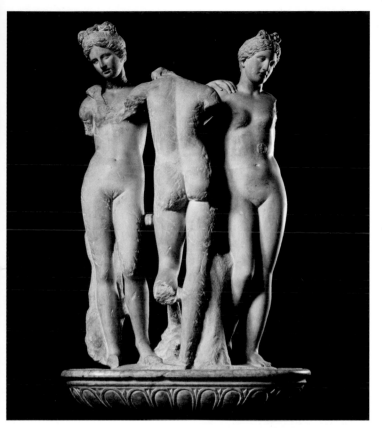

*Ceiling with grotesques*

Three Graces, *sculptural group from the Roman Era*

to ornament the Library in 1502. Giovanni di Stefano sculpted the base in marble and decorated it in a clear archaeological style with gargoyles which subsequently became fundamental elements of his repertoire, while the trunk of the column, to honour the family, is decorated with a motif of Piccolominian moons.

The floor also contains the Piccolomini family symbol in a rather obsessive manner. Ornamental blue majolica tiles in triangular shapes with a gold half moon on them originally formed the paving but it was completely redone in the nineteenth century using rhomboid ornamental tiles from the Ginori Manufacture in Florence.

Display cases made from ancient chairs carved by Antonio Barili (1495–1496) line the walls. They contain a series of thirty choir books made between 1465 and 1515 and constitute one of the most conspicuous treasures of

Renaissance miniatures in Italy. These large parchment music books are subdivided according to their liturgical purpose. The *Antiphonaries* contain the day and night prayers of the Divine Office and the *Graduals* contain the sung parts of Mass.

Various people were involved in decorating these precious volumes including the Sienese artists Sano di Pietro, Pellegrino di Mariano, Benvenuto di Giovanni and Guidoccio Cozzarelli. In addition to these artists two other people worked on the volumes, Liberale da Verona and Girolamo da Cremona. These men triggered the renewal of Sienese painting in the second half of the fifteenth century and created refined miniatures characterised by ingenious compositional innovation, vivid and bright colours and rich and exuberant ornamentation.

*Pellegrino di Mariano,* Vocation of St. Peter and St. Paul, *Antiphonary 11. M, c. 4*

*Girolamo da Cremona,* Isaiah's Vision, *Antiphonary 1. A, c. 4v*

*Liberale da Verona,* Parable of the beam and two blind men, *Gradual 24.9, c. 1*

*Francesco Rosselli and Liberale da Verona, Gradual 25.10, cc. 61v-62 with the* Woman Healed of her Hemorrhage

Cathedral - Piccolomini Library

# Choir

Francesco del Tonghio started work on the ancient gothic choir in 1362 and over time various artists joined him, such as his son Giacomo (1378) and the carver Mariano d'Angelo Romanelli (1386). Surviving documentation informs us that this magnificent piece of wood carving was made up of ninety stalls positioned in a double row, dominated by baldachins and decorated with full-length statues. Unfortunately only 36 stalls with their banisters and kneeling-stools remain. These stalls sit under small acute arches which contain the formerly polychrome busts of saints and prophets made during the first half of the fifteenth century. A radical transformation of the choir took place during the second half of the sixteenth century when the apsidal niche behind the altar was opened out and the Opera decided to position a new choir there. The rector of the Opera, Marcello Tegliacci, entrusted the task to Bartolomeo Neroni known as Riccio. Riccio received a preliminary payment for the design of the new choir in 1567. Unfortunately the artist died only a few years later (1571) and his collaborators carried out the construction of his fabulous design. The result is a masterpiece of sixteenth-century carving where the work's extraordinarily fine and masterful execution combines with beautiful decorative magnificence. The same artists, also from a design by Riccio, made the wonderful lectern (1573) in the centre of the semicircle behind the main altar and the resident *in cornu epistolae* (1575) accompanied by a rich repertoire of late sixteenth-century figures such as winged victories, harpies, gargoyles, candelabras, flowers, vases and little putti.

Another important transformation of the choir took place during the second decade of the nineteenth century. In 1813, at the desire of the then archbishop of Siena, Antonio Felice Zondadari, thirty-eight inlaid panels from the abbey of Monte Oliveto Maggiore were positioned on the backrests of the ancient fourteenth-century stalls. They were made between 1503 and 1505 by Fra Giovanni da Verona. The intarsia portray cityscapes and structures separated by faux wardrobes with half-open doors which contain books, liturgical furnishings and musical instruments. The effects of perspective and the daring foreshortening of the depicted objects are extraordinary and the evocative landscapes are brought to life by

*Fra Giovanni da Verona,* Cabinet with liturgical furnishings, *wooden inlay*

*Fra Giovanni da Verona,* Rural landscape with a rabbit, *wooden inlay*

*Fra Giovanni da Verona,* View of a central-plan temple, *wooden inlay*

*Fra Giovanni da Verona,* Cabinet with a basket of grapes and liturgical books, *wooden inlay*

wild rabbits and birds with multi-coloured plumage by the refined use of chiaroscuro techniques. In actual fact the artist had developed a certain craftsmanship with the art of marquetry which led him to use different coloured wood, dying it when necessary with sulphur and verdigris to get resplendent iridescent tones.

# Sacristy

At the beginning of the fifteenth century the need to build a new sacristy became apparent, one which was more beautiful and worthy of the magnificent cathedral. The master mason at the time, Caterino di Corsino, passed on a request to the Comune of Siena to obtain a licence for the new construction work. He proposed that the Comune buy some of the houses in Via dei Fusari and connect them to the walls of the cathedral with a vault which would pass over the road itself. The licence was granted and between 1408 and 1409 the construction work on the new sacristy was planned. At the far end of the large room there are three vaulted chapels frescoed by Benedetto di Bindo in 1412. The first chapel on the right is known as the "dei Liri" or "dei Libri" chapel (Chapel of Books) and in actual fact books were kept there to be used by the clergy during rites. It contains frescoes depicting the *Triumph of Faith over Heresy* and *Evangelists and Doctors of the Church*. In the centre of the middle chapel there is an altar with a sixteenth-century painting by Francesco Rustici depicting the *Dead Christ* and some scenes of the *Life of the Virgin* by Benedetto di Bindo. The left-hand chapel is known as the chapel of the reliquaries because the relics of saints were kept there inside special cabinets called "Arliquiere". The chapel contains paintings of the *Apparition of the Madonna* and the *Apparition of St. Michael at Castel Sant'Angelo, saints and prophets*. Benedetto di Bindo also made doors for these cabinets in this chapel in the same year. These depict *Angels* and *Stories of the True Cross* and are currently in the Museo dell'Opera. The relics cabinets along the walls of this room contain precious liturgical objects in gilded copper, silver and gold along with a precious collection of sacred vestments which are among the most important in Italy.

The remains of a fresco done between 1435 and 1440 by Domenico di Bartolo with *Stories of the Four Patron Saints of Siena* can be seen on the entrance wall of the sacristy, while an elegant holy-water stoup sits beside the door. The stoup was made in 1437 by Giovanni Turini and shows an angel in gilded bronze holding up an enamel cup decorated with coats of arms and inscriptions.

---

*Benedetto di Bindo, Frescoes, chapel of the reliquaries*

*Benedetto di Bindo, "Arliquiera", Museo dell'Opera*

# Stained Glass Windows

The desire to fill cathedrals with coloured light through harmonious, elegant windows enriched with decorated glass originated from an instinctive impulse on the part of the earliest builders of sacred structures. Through the transparency of the glass panes they thought it would be possible to create such a strong, evocative religious impression that worshipers would be able to come even closer to understanding the divine word. Hence, from the thirteenth century onwards, the increasing presence in Siena of entire families of stained glass window masters. These artists drew inspiration from the great French school beyond the Alps which was capable of creating work of unimaginable beauty.

Siena Cathedral, however, does not contain a single style of window. The difference between the two large circular windows on the façade and the apse and the ones along the central nave and around the dome is very obvious.

In the nineteenth century Milanesi maintained that the large, circular stained glass window on the apse was the work of Iacopo del Castello but in 1946 Enzo Carli linked it to Duccio di Buoninsegna.

It was made between 1287 and 1290 and a document has been found dated 1287 which deliberates and concludes that the *finestra rotunda magna* above the main altar should be supplied with a stained glass pane. This window, along with the *Maestà*, is undoubtedly Duccio di Buoninsegna's most important work and by far one of the most important in Italy, reaching six

metres across and covering thirty metres squared. Proceeding from the bottom upwards, the central section depicts three scenes from the stories of the Virgin: *the Burial*, *the Assumption* and the *Coronation*. The four *Evangelists* are depicted in the triangles while the horizontal section contains the four patron saints of Siena in pairs: *St. Bartholomew*, *St. Ansanus*, *St. Crescentius* and *St. Savinus*. It is interesting to note that St. Bartholomew was

*Duccio di Buoninsegna,* Assumption of the Virgin, *apsidal stained glass window detail, Museo dell'Opera*

*Duccio di Buoninsegna,* St. Ansanus, *apsidal stained glass window detail, Museo dell'Opera*

already considered to be one of the patron saints of the town as he had replaced St. Victor at the beginning of the fourteenth century. The message of salvation which emerges from this complex iconography was ultimately intended to give faith and hope to the citizens. The *Stained Glass Window* along with the *Maestà* which used to be under it on the main altar became the keystone of Sienese religious sensibilities.

The scenes convey the gentle style of narration typical of Duccio, especially the pane with the *Coronation* where angels with delicately inclined heads surround the throne and seem to anticipate those on the great altarpiece.

*Duccio di Buoninsegna*, Apsidal stained glass window, *Museo dell'Opera*

*Pastorino de' Pastorini*, Stained glass window, *façade*

The bright and vivid colours are also typical of Duccio's style. The intense blue of the backgrounds, the golden yellow, ruby red, amethyst purple and emerald green of the clothes together with the delicate pink of the flesh shine brightly with an extraordinary chromatic effect. The true innovation of this work, however, is the presence of "grisaille". Duccio personally used the fine filaments of his brush to add colour to the glass panes and highlight the details on the faces, the drapery and the angels' wings. The large stained glass window has been substituted with a copy and the original can be seen in its entirety in the ground floor room of the Museo dell'Opera.

The façade, on the other hand, holds a stained glass window with the *Last Supper* made in 1549 by Pastorino de' Pastorini. Pastorini was a pupil of Guillaume de Marcillat, the French clergyman and artist who was skilful in the art of glass making and made some of the most beautiful stained glass windows of the sixteenth century for Arezzo Cathedral. Pastorini designed the whole of the Sienese window with magnificent classicism with the people dressed in mantles overflowing with colour on a background of imposing structures in light glass panes. The coat of arms of the rector who commissioned the work from the artist, Azzolino de' Cerretani, is visible at the bottom in the centre along with the artist's name and the date.

The two stained glass windows either side of the main altar in the Chapel of the Sacrament and the Chapel of St. Ansanus respectively are also worthy of praise. The windows were originally part of a single work in a double lancet window in the abolished convent of St. Francis at Colle Val d'Elsa and came to the Cathedral as part of a donation from the town council at the end of the nineteenth century (1885). The windows depict *St. Bonaventure*, *St. Bernardine* and *St. Luke* (right) and *St. Francis*, *St. Biagio* and *St. Anthony of Padua* (left).

During the restoration work in the cathedral between 1881 and 1889, the windows along the main nave were opened up and replaced with simple clear glass panes. These panes hold the coats of arms of the public and private institutions which funded the work as well as the images of popes descended from Sienese families. In contrast, the twelve new windows around the tambour of the dome were made in coloured glass by Ulisse de Matteis in 1886 from a design by Alessandro Franchi. They depict the twelve *Apostles*, each one with their iconographical attributes and a book marked with a cross as a symbol of their evangelical purpose.

Floor

The most beautiful, "great and magnificent paving ever made". This is how Giorgio Vasari described Siena cathedral's paving in his *Lives of the most eminent painters, sculptors and architects*. The task of decorating the floor began in the fourteenth century (the first evidence of work can be traced to 1369). It was worked on by anonymous artists and was not completed until the nineteenth century with the help of artists from the Institute of Fine Arts. The preparatory drawings for the fifty-six scenes were done by various artists who had all studied in Siena (among others Sassetta, Domenico di Bartolo, Matteo di Giovanni, Francesco di Giorgio Martini and Domenico Beccafumi) except the inlay depicting the *Allegory of the Hill of Knowledge*. This was drawn by the Umbrian artist Bernardino di Betto known as Pinturicchio between 1505 and 1506 while he was decorating the Piccolomini Library. The floor was made using the marble "commesso" technique and "graffito". It was started in a simple fashion then gradually reached surprising perfection, so much so that the tarsia seem like they are part of a pictorial work with multiple chromatic gradations. The first tarsia were hatched over white marble slabs with grooves made by scalpels and drills then filled in with black stucco. This technique is called "graffito". Subsequently coloured pieces of marble were placed next to each other to form the marble "commesso" in the same way as a wooden intarsia. Later on artists were able to combine the two techniques of graffito and commesso. Domenico Beccafumi, a Sienese mannerist painter from the first half of the sixteenth century, perfected the marble commesso technique even further and was able to obtain extraordinary, quite evocative pictorial chiaroscuro effects. The only panel made as a mosaic instead of a commesso was the *Sienese wolf with symbols of other towns* in the central nave by Leopoldo Maccari (1864-1865). This was a nineteenth century reconstruction of a fifteenth century original, some fragments of which are kept in the Museo dell'Opera.

Collectively the ornamentation and panels which spread over the entire floor of the cathedral became a masterpiece of unmistakeable character and unparalleled beauty, a unique and unsurpassable example of Italian art.

The floor embodies an actual doctrinal text which reveals a complex account made through allegoric, civil, mythological, philosophical and theological religious motifs from the old and new testaments. The story progresses from pagan antiquity, through the figures of *Hermes Trigmegistus* and those of the ten *Sibyls* who foretold the coming of the Redeemer, and touches on the story of the elected People (*Stories of Moses*), until it comes to the episodes about the town of Siena. It is a long narrative set in stone which accompanies the Revelation of Christ throughout the stages of the story of man.

The extraordinary marble commesso technique on the cathedral's floor came to be appreciated in a new public and religious light and was used a great deal well into the nineteenth century and beyond. It helped bring the marvel of masterly artisanal skill and knowledge of more sophisticated, minute techniques to a wider audience. Otherwise, the genre would have been labelled by art historians as an oddity which stemmed from the capricious temperament of some buyer or eccentric artist. The people of Siena, however, proved to be particularly receptive to the charm of the sculpted intarsia and the town enthusiastically welcomed suggestions for the "paintings in stone" inside the cathedral.

Every one of the fifty-six scenes is worthy of a stylistic description and an in-depth, detailed critique but there are too many to fully analyse here. The following list provides the key information about each section and its position on the cathedral floor. In 1884 Giovanni Paciarelli drew the whole floor with all its decorative sections. This large drawing can currently be seen in the Museo dell'Opera.

---

*Giovanni Paciarelli,* Floor layout of the Cathedral, *1884, Museo dell'Opera*

# Floor Layout

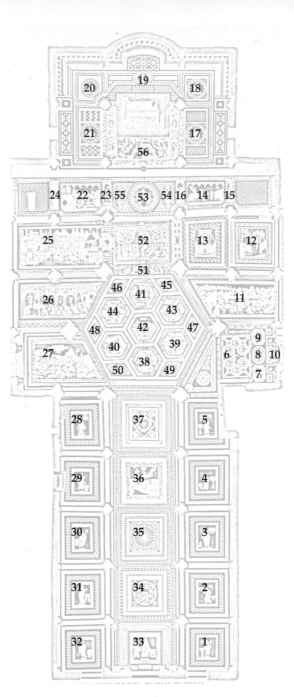

1. Attributed to Giovanni di Stefano or Antonio Federighi, *Delphic Sibyl* (1482)

2. Giovanni di Stefano, *Cimmerian Sibyl* (1482)

3. Giovanni di Stefano, *Cumean Sibyl* (1482)

4. Antonio Federighi, *Erythraean Sibyl* (1482)

5. Attribuito a Urbano da Cortona or Benvenuto di Giovanni, *Persian Sibyl* (1482)

6. Antonio Federighi, *Seven Ages of Man* (1475)

7. Leopoldo Maccari from a design by Alessandro Franchi, *Hope* (1875–1878)

8. Leopoldo Maccari from a design by Alessandro Franchi, *Faith* (1875–1878)

9. Leopoldo Maccari from a design by Alessandro Franchi, *Charity* (1875–1878)

10. Leopoldo Maccari from a design by Alessandro Franchi, *Religion* (1875–1878)

11. Francesco di Giorgio Martini, *Stories of Jephthah* (1483)

12. Pietro del Minnella, *Death of Absalom* (1447)

13. Domenico di Bartolo, *Emperor Sigismund* (1434)

14. Stefano di Giovanni known as Sassetta, *Samson destroys the Philistines* (1426)

15. Domenico di Niccolò dei Cori, *Judas Maccabeus* (1424)

16. *Moses* (1426)

17. Attributed to Martino di Bartolomeo and Taddeo di Bartolo, *Temperance* (1406)

18. Attributed to Martino di Bartolomeo and Taddeo di Bartolo, *Prudence* (1406)

19. Attributed to Martino di Bartolomeo and Taddeo di Bartolo, *Mercy* (1406)

20. Attributed to Martino di Bartolomeo and Taddeo di Bartolo, *Justice* (1406)

21. Attributed to Martino di Bartolomeo and Taddeo di Bartolo, *Fortitude* (1406)

22. Stefano di Giovanni known as Sassetta, *Joshua defeats the five Amorite kings* (1426)

23. *Joshua* (1426)

24. *Solomon* (1426)

25. Francesco di Giorgio Martini, *Stories of Judith* (1473)

26. Matteo di Giovanni, *Slaughter of the Innocents* (1481)

27. Benvenuto di Giovanni, *Expulsion of Herod* (1484)

28. Benvenuto di Giovanni, *Albunea Sibyl* (1483)

29. Matteo di Giovanni, *Samian Sibyl* (1483)

30. Benvenuto di Giovanni (?), *Phrygian Sibyl* (1483)

31. Neroccio di Bartolomeo, *Hellespontine Sibyl* (1483)

32. Guidoccio Cozzarelli, *Libyan Sibyl*, (1483)

33. Giovanni di Stefano, *Hermes Trismegistus* (1488)

34. Leopoldo Maccari (from a 14th-century original), *Wolf suckling Romulus and Remus*

35. *Wheel with imperial eagle*, 19th-century copy of a 14th-century original

36. Bernardino di Betto known as Pinturicchio, *Allegory of the Mount of Knowledge* (1505-1506)

37. Leopoldo Maccari from a design by Luigi Mussini (from a 14th-century original), *Wheel of Fortune*

38. Alessandro Franchi, *Ascension of Elijah on a chariot of fire*

39. Alessandro Franchi, *Elijah predicts the death in battle of Ahab*

40. Alessandro Franchi, *Death of Ahab*

41. Domenico Beccafumi, *Sacrifice of Elijah* (1518–1524)

42. Domenico Beccafumi, *Meeting of Elijah and Ahab* (1518–1524)

43. Domenico Beccafumi, *Murder of the prophets of Baal* (1518–1524)

44. Domenico Beccafumi, *Sacrifice of Ahab* (1518–1524)

45. Domenico Beccafumi, *Abdias and Elijah* (1518–1524)

46. Domenico Beccafumi, *Ahab and Abdias* (1518–1524)

47. Alessandro Franchi, *Elijah fed by crows* (1875–1878)

48. Alessandro Franchi, *Elijah oils Jehu, king of Israel* (1875–1878)

49. Alessandro Franchi, *Meeting of Elijah with the widow* (1875–1878)

50. Alessandro Franchi, *Elijah resuscitates the widow's son* (1875–1878)

51. Domenico Beccafumi, *Moses makes water gush from the rock* (1525)

52. Domenico Beccafumi, *Stories of Moses on Mount Sinai* (1531)

53. Attributed to Domenico di Niccolò dei Cori and Giovanni di Francesco da Imola, *King David Psalmist* (1424)

54. Attributed to Domenico di Niccolò dei Cori and Giovanni di Francesco da Imola, *The Giant Goliath* (1424)

55. Attributed to Domenico di Niccolò dei Cori and Giovanni di Francesco da Imola, *David the slinger* (1424)

56. Domenico Beccafumi, *Sacrifice of Abraham* (1544–1547)

IN CIBVM FEL INSITVM ACE
TVM DEDERVNT HANC
IN HOSPITALITATIS NOSTRA
ABVNT MENSAM TEMPLI
VERO SONDIETVR VELVM
ET MEDIO DIE NOX ERIT
TENEBROSA TRIBVS HORIS

SIBYLLA HELLESPONTICA IN A
GRO TROIANO NATA QVA SCRIBIT
HERACLIDES CYRI TEPORE FVISSE

INMANVS INIQVA
VENIET. DABVNT DEO
ALAPAS MANIBVS IN
CERTIS. MISERABILIS
ET IGNOMINIOSVS
MISERABILIBVS SPEM
PRAEBEBIT.

SIBYLLA LYBICA
CVIVS MEMINIT
EVRIPIDES

*Pietro del Minnella*, Death of Absolom *(12)*

*Giovanni di Stefano*, Hermes Trismegistus *(33)*

*Leopoldo Maccari (from a 14th-century original)*, Wolf suckling Romulus and Remus *(34)*

*Pinturicchio*, Allegory of the Hill of Knowledge *(36)*

SE NA
FLORENTIA
AROTIVM
PISA
TUS

SOCRATES
HVC PROPERATE VIRI
SALEBROSVM SCANDITE
MONTEM
PVLCHRA LABORIS ERVNT
PREMIA PALMA QVIDE
CRATES

*Domenico Beccafumi,* Moses makes water gush from the rock, *detail (51)*

*Domenico Beccafumi,* Stories of Moses on Mount Sinai, *detail (52)*

*Domenico Beccafumi,* Pagan Sacrifice, *detail of the Sacrifice of Abrham (56)*

*Matteo di Giovanni,* Slaughter of the Innocents *(26) and detail*

# Crypt

The room which is commonly known as the Crypt was redis-covered in its present condition in 1999 following a restoration project on the structure of the Cathedral.

We know that there was original-ly a church under the cathedral which had a façade with three large gateways facing the town centre. This area was connected to the church above by two stair-ways which emerged straight under the dome through the hex-agonal floor panel. It is thought that the rediscovered room could have been part of the church un-derneath and was in all likewood a "confession" as it was situated right against the back façade of the thirteenth-century cathedral. During the fourteenth century however, extensive renovations changed the appearance and purpose of the crypt. In actual fact, expansion work to the Ca-thedral's choir began in 1317 and led to the inevitable dismantle-ment of the cross vaulting while the construction of the new bap-tistery brought about the destruc tion of this large room's façade. Subsequently, the crypt became a simple storeroom for debris from various renovation projects inside the metropolitan church.

Now, about seven centuries later, we have the chance to see part of the old structure of the lower church whose walls are covered in a series of perfectly conserved and extraordinarily beautiful mu-ral paintings from around 1280. This cycle of frescoes constitutes

an important piece of evidence of the existence of a Sienese school of fresco masters working in the last quarter of the thirteenth cen-tury. They included Dietisalvi di Speme, Guido di Graziano and Rinaldo da Siena, assisted by a very young Duccio di Buon-insegna who almost certainly participated in this magnificent venture.

The narration of the scenes starts on the far wall from the cur-rent entrance and continues in a clockwise direction around the perimeter. The story unfolds on two parallel rows but the upper row has almost entirely been lost because of the demolition of the vaults. It held *Stories from the Old Testament* whereas the lower row held *Stories from the New Testa-ment*. Three splendid scenes depicting the *Crucifixion*, the *Deposition from the Cross* and the *Deposition in the Tomb* are worth mentioning. They are character-ised by vibrant reds, deep blues and glittering golds. This intense chromatic range was also used in the geometric designs on various architectural elements such as the bases of the columns, the half pil-lars and the capitals.

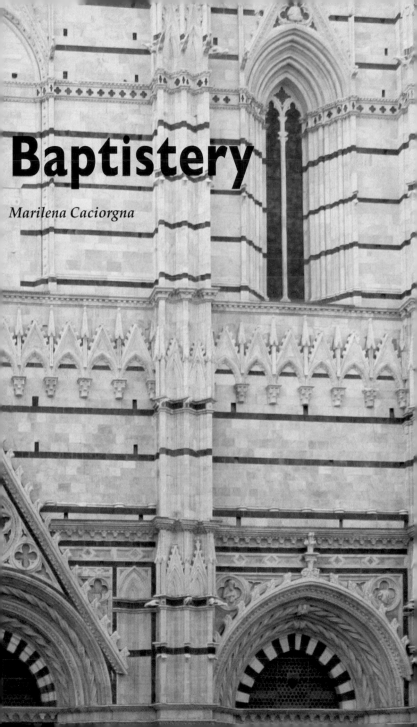

# Baptistery

*Marilena Caciorgna*

Visitors who turn into Via dei Pellegrini from Piazza del Campo and pass by the Magnifico Pandolfo Petrucci Palace will then find themselves, after a hilly climb, in front of the Parish Church of San Giovanni. The Church was built in an almost "crypt-like" position under the Cathedral. It is possible that the construction work was overseen by Camaino di Crescentino, master mason from 1299 onwards as Giovanni Pisano had already left Siena (he was probably already back in Pisa by 1297). A marble façade towers above onlookers in the small square below which bears the same name as the Church. This imposing prospect should have been the rear wall of the Cathedral facing the town centre but after the construction work it not only hid the façade of the Baptistery, it also concealed the choir of the "old" enlarged cathedral. From the choir area the enormous circle which held Duccio di Buoninsegna's stained glass window can be seen. The original window was substituted with a copy in May 2007 and is now in the Museo dell'Opera (Galleria delle Statue).

On the 23rd August 1339 the Consiglio Generale della Campana sanctioned the decision to enlarge the Sienese cathedral. The existing church would have become the transept of the new cathedral and the naves would have gone along the current Piazza Jacopo della Quercia. In actual fact, work on the enlargement to the east (Vallepiatta) and construction work on the Baptistery's façade had begun on the 1st May 1317.

According to the plans kept in the Archive of the Opera Metropolitana of Siena (drawings in pen and brown ink on vellum), the main body of the Church of San Giovanni, the marble façade and the sculptures in the gateways had been completed by the time the vaulting was closed up in June 1325.

From 1348 onwards construction work on the so-called "New Cathedral" suffered significant delays until it was definitively suspended. This was because of both the economic recession caused by the Black Death and the statics problems found in some parts

*The inside of the Baptistery with the Baptismal Font and the old altar before restoration work took place in the second half of the 19th century, photograph from c. 1870*

*Façade*

of the building. Up until now historians have maintained that between 1339 and 1348 the only work still in progress was on the construction of the naves and the "Great Façade" ("Facciatone") of the "New Cathedral". Work on the façade of the Bapistery on the other hand, had been abandoned. It was only during the 1360s that construction work proceeded on the middle section where three windows can be seen above the gateways. The most recent critiques, however, maintain that during the expansion work on the cathedral, around the time when the sculptor Giovanni d'Agostino was master mason of the Opera di Santa Maria, work continued on the Baptistery's façade. This was from 1340 until 1348, probably the year in which the artist died from the plague.

In actual fact the reliefs in the Gothic pediments of the church's windows depicting *Christ benedictory*, *St. Apollonia* and a *Prophet* can be traced back to Giovanni d'Agostino's work in the 1340s. The originals have been temporarily replaced by copies (they have just been restored and are ready to be repositioned). The same artist also sculpted the busts that decorate the Gothic pediments of the windows on the side of the Baptistery (two on the left hand side and one on the right of which the copies are visible). These sculptures, characterised by elegant Gothic stylistic features, are similar to the figures created by Simone Martini for his pictorial work.

The gateway which opens onto the right-hand nave of the "new cathedral" is also believed to be the work of Giovanni d'Agostino. *Christ benedictory between two angels* is depicted there and it can be seen from Piazza San Giovanni at the top of the spectacular flight of steps. The original statues from the

*Giovanni d'Agostino, Gateway of the New Cathedral*

*Giovanni d'Agostino,* St. Apollonia, *Museo dell'Opera, in storage*

*Giovanni d'Agostino,* Christ benedictory with two angels, *Museo dell'Opera*

marble sculptural group are in the Sala degli Apostoli inside the Museo dell'Opera.

On the pendentives of the small crowning arches further up the incomplete façade there are eight womanly and virile human heads sculpted with considerable expressionism and originality. They were completed during the 1350s and early 1360s as work on the façade was abandoned in 1365. It has been suggested that they were done by Giovanni d'Agostino's brother, Domenico d'Agostino. He was also a sculptor and architect and took up the position of master mason of Siena cathedral after his brother's death.

On the pavement of the parvis in front of the three gateways we can admire the inlays done using the marble "commesso" technique and the graffito depicting *Birth*, *Baptism* and *Confirmation* which are suggestive of this sacred place's purpose. The two scenes on each side were commissioned in 1450 from Bartolomeo di Mariano known as Mandriano, perhaps based on a design by Nastagio di Guasparre. The middle one was finished five years later by Antonio Federighi, the artist who made various other "commessi" designs for the cathedral's floor (the inlay work has been repeatedly restored and is quite worn down).

*Domenico d'Agostino (?)*, Virile head, *Museo dell'Opera, in storage*

*Domenico d'Agostino (?)*, Feminine head, *Museo dell'Opera, in storage*

# Frescoes in the Bays

As soon as visitors enter the church they find themselves in a rectangular area divided into three naves by two large pillars. Each nave is made up of two bays with cross vaults marked out by groins. The frescoes almost completely cover the inside of the Baptistery and along with the art work in the *Pellegrinaio* of Santa Maria della Scala they constitute some of the most illustrative examples of Sienese art of the fifteenth century. The webs of the vaults adjacent to the counter-façade featuring the *Apostles* were painted first. The two lateral vaults are thought to be the work of Agostino di Marsiglio, a Bolognese artist who started his career at the Baptistery under Michele di Matteo Lambertini (notes from 1410 to 1469). The central vault also features the apostles and was frescoed by Lorenzo di Pietro known as Vecchietta. On the 7th February 1450 he was asked by the Opera della Metropolitana to "draw up plans for the Church […], or chapel of St. John for its vaults, sides and walls". Vecchietta (1410-1480) studied in the Sienese milieu even though he was influenced by Florentine art as he had worked with Masolino da Panicale at Castiglione Olona. He was a versatile artist, painter, sculptor and architect; when he signed his work he called himself a "painter" on sculptures and a "sculptor" on paintings, almost as if he wanted to make a name for himself in both artistic genres.

In the first vault on the left *St. James the Elder* can be seen with the pilgrim's staff next to *St. Andrew* with the cross, *St. Bartholomew* with the knife and *St. Peter* with the keys. In the central vault we can see *St. James the Younger* between *Hope* with its hands and face turned upwards and *Faith* holding the cross, *St. Matthew* between *Fortitude* with the column and *Knowledge*; *St. Philip* between *Constancy* with the column and *Perseverance* with the sword, and *St. John* between *Charity* and *Truth* with the mirror. The Apostles in the vault on the right are no longer identifiable either by their attributes or by their inscriptions but they are thought to be what is left of *Thomas, Jude Thaddeus, Simon the Zealot* and *Matthew*.

Besides doing the frescoes on the central vault near the entrance Vecchietta also decorated the three bays near the far wall with the *Articles of the Creed*. This subject was quite uncommon in Italian art but documentary evidence of some lost works suggests it became very popular in Siena from the fourteenth century onwards. Furthermore, Vecchietta had already used the *Creed* as subject matter. The frescoes on the Sacrestia Grande of Santa Maria della Scala, also known as the Cappella del Sacro Chiodo or the Cappella del Manto, can be traced back to 1449. There the artist depicted the *Apostolic Symbol* in the lunettes and some *Biblical Stories* in the rectangles below. This was a series of scenes with quite complex iconography and they are difficult to decipher because of their fragmentary state. The *Creed* depicted in the Baptistery does not correspond to the Nicene Creed (recited during

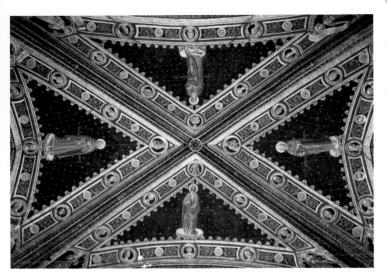

Mass) but rather to the more concise version of the Apostolic Symbol according to a doctrine conceived in all likelihood by an expert in theology. By the term Apostolic Symbol the Fathers of the Church denoted the rule or profession of faith required to become baptised. Its portrayal is therefore well-suited to its location.

There are twelve scenes with the *Articles of the Creed*, four for each bay proceeding in an anticlockwise direction. Each web of the cross vaults containing an *Article* features an apostle in the bottom right corner and a prophet in the bottom left corner. They can be identified by the writing next to the various figures and the inscriptions on the cartouches. In a sermon attributed to Pseudo-Saint Augustine which was considered to be authentic in the Middle Ages, each Apostle was assigned with an article of the Creed. There is also a perfect correlation between the number of disciples of Christ and the number of articles in the Apostolic Symbol.

Besides the *Articles* Vecchietta did some of the decorative work on the frames of the webs. In the second bay the ornamental motifs are formed by acanthus swirls, supplely shaped putti filling the perspectival niches, ocula in which figurative profiles are depicted and elegant portraits. The series is subdivided by a sequence of figures including prophets, the Eritrean Sibyl, various Virtues and some allegories to inspire the public like *Peace* and *Goodwill* which seem to be based on Ambrogio Lorenzetti's *Good Government*. The presence of *Peace* in the series in the Sacristy of the Santa Maria della Scala hospital is also significant.

*Lorenzo di Pietro, known as Vecchietta,* Apostles, *central vault*

## ■ Articles in the First Bay

I. Proceeding in an anticlockwise direction around the first bay, the first four Articles of the Creed painted by Vecchietta are silhouetted against a starry, cobalt blue sky. In the web next to the left-hand wall of St. John's Church we can see the first revealed truth from the Creed, that is *Credo in Deum, Patrem omnipotentem, creatorem caeli et terrae* (I believe in God, the Father almighty, creator of heaven and earth), illustrated by an image of the Eternal with His right hand raised towards the sky. The left hand is no longer visible because of the fresco's deterioration but it is probable that it pointed towards the ground. Immersed in a sphere of light symbolising the earth, God appears to be represented as the creator of all things celestial and all things earthly. He intends to show us the empyrean with one hand and the earth with the other, a typology which is persistently recurrent in Sienese cycles featuring the *Creed*. On the left of God the Father there is a faithful follower on his knees with his hands clasped together as he recites the Creed. There are other faithful followers depicted in the same position in each web of the vault. Apart from the scene of the first article where the letters have fallen away, the webs all contain the word "CREED" in capital letters next to the mouth of the man.

From the iconography in the next two bays and partly in the first bay, the viewer can expect to see an apostle in the bottom right corner of the webs and a prophet on the left, each with their own phylactery and inscription. The apostle in the first scene should thus be Peter who, according to Pseudo-Saint Augustine, is reciting the first article of the Creed. Due to the distinctive features of this figure, however, we must exclude the possibility of it being Peter. The inscription on the cartouche is difficult to decipher as the writing does not correspond to any script from either the Medieval or the Humanistic era. Not even the *titulus* of the figure on the left of the web is legible. It is thought that the partially damaged ancient inscriptions were not taken into consideration during the restoration of the frescoes. The unskilled restorers used marks and abbreviations characteristic of Gothic writing instead, without any reference to the original. The same thing happened to the inscription relating to the figure in the bottom left corner of the second web and also in part to the *titulus* relating to St. John the Evangelist.

II. The scene next to the far wall features the second article of faith as written in the inscription on the phylactery ET IN IESUM CHRISTUM FILIUM EIUS UNICUM DOMINUM NOSTRUM (and in Jesus Christ, his only Son, our Lord). The illustration of the Apostolic Symbol as regards Jesus Christ begins here. He is depicted facing us, the wound on his chest visible under his cloak. The article is pronounced by Andrew (ANDREAS in the inscription) following Pseudo-Saint Augustine's writings.

III. The cartouche inscription pointed out by St. James the Elder (S. JACOBUS) in the third web reads QUI CONCETTUS EST DE SPIRITU SANCTO, NATUS EX MARIA VIRGINE (who was conceived by the power of the Holy Spirit, born of the Virgin Mary). The scene represents the Annunciation of the Incarnation of the Word made to Mary by the archangel Gabriel using a typology which can be seen in almost all the cycles featuring the Creed. The article pronounced by James follows Pseudo-Saint Augustine's writings.

On the other side Isaiah (YSAIAS), one of the four major prophets, declares ECCE VIRGO CONCIPIET ET PARIET FILIUM (The virgin will be with child and will give birth to a son), a famous prophesy which is well known in liturgy and can be found in the Book of Isaiah 7:14. This revealed truth is depicted according to the traditional iconography of the Annunciation from the Gospel of Luke (1:34) which was quite well known in the Middle Ages and the Renaissance. The lyricism of the scene is conveyed through the simplicity of the porticoed area where light, transparent drapes are silhouetted in the background. The archangel Gabriel, messenger of God, is on his knees in front of the Virgin who, in the words of

Simone Martini, is drawn back in a gesture which demonstrates her reserve and humility.

IV. In the fourth and last web the Passion and death of Christ can be seen: *Passus sub Pontio Pilato, crucifixus, mortuus, et sepultus* (suffered under Pontius Pilate, was crucified, died, and was buried). The article is expressed here by the apostle and evangelist John who is identified by the inscription S. IOHANNES EVAN[GELISTA]. The incipit, PASSUS, can be seen clearly but the subsequent words are much more difficult to make out.

Parallel to John the Evangelist, Ezekiel pronounces his prophesy: SIGNA THAU GE[ME]NTIUM which refers to a passage from his book (9:4; 6). According to a venerable tradition widely supported in patristic circles, the form of the Greek letter tau corresponds to the form of a cross. This passage from Ezekiel is thus interpreted as a reference to the salvation of mankind through the sacrifice of Christ.

The three parts of the Passion can be seen in the web: the *Flagellation*, the *Crucifixion* and the *Burial*. The first part of these three episodes dominates the scene. Christ is bound to a Corinthian column in the centre of the composition and beaten while Pilate watches from his seat on the faldstool. The laurel wreath on his head symbolises his authority. The Crucifix in the architectural aedicule at the top of the scene stands out against

the starry sky while the *Burial* is represented on a smaller scale in the right-hand corner of the web. Christ is placed in the sarcophagus wrapped in bandages; this is a persistently recurring image in cycles featuring the *Creed*.

*Lorenzo di Pietro, known as Vecchietta,*
Articles of the Creed. Annunciation
(Qui conceptus est de Spiritu Sancto,
natus ex Maria Virgine), *1ˢᵗ bay, 3ʳᵈ web*

## ■ Articles in the Second Bay

V. In the second bay, following the iconographic pattern, we come to the fifth web. The scenes *Christ in Limbo* and *Resurrection* are portrayed here according to the dictates of the Creed: *descendit ad inferos; tertia die resurrexit a mortuis* (He descended into hell. On the third day he rose again from the dead). At the bottom of the scene Christ bears the fruit of redemption to the souls of the just who were born at a time when the benefit of the sacraments was not known to people.

Crowded into a cavernous cave, the dead people come forward and turn their piteous faces towards the Saviour. The patriarchs can be seen among them. Adam is depicted as an old man with a long, grey beard, leaning forward to form a bow with his hand reaching out to Christ while Eve is on her knees with her arms folded. On the right John the Baptist is dressed in animal skins and a purple cloak as he points with his left hand to a cartouche with the motto "Ecce Agnus Dei" from the forth Gospel (John 1:36). John on the other hand, is the link between the Old and New Testaments as he is considered to be the last of the prophets of the Old Testament and the first saint of the New Testament. In actual fact, contrary to the other souls in Limbo, he appears to have a halo. On the left the devil has just come out of the door to Hades and at the top of the scene the *Resurrection* is depicted. Christ is standing on his marble, half open grave with a flag with a red cross in his hand.

Theological explanations and iconographic forms are also recurrent here with aspects similar to those in the Sacrestia dello Spedale.

Following the same iconographic pattern the apostle Thomas (TOMAS on the cartouche) can be seen in the bottom right corner saying DESCENDIT AD INFEROS TERTIA DIE RESURREXIT A MORTUIS (He descended into hell. On the third day he rose again from the dead.) On the other side Hosea (OSEA in the inscription) pronounces MORSUS TUUS ERO INFERNE which refers to a sentence in the prophet's book (13:14) *O mors ero mors tua, morsus tuus ero, inferne* (O death, I will be thy plagues; O grave, I will be thy destruction). The source which connects Thomas to the descent into the Netherworld and the Resurrection postulated in the Creed is, yet again, Pseudo-Saint Augustine.

VI. The representation of the Apostolic Symbol continues with the Ascension as heralded by James the Younger (IACOBUS in the inscription): ASCEN[DIT IN] CELUM SEDET AD DEXTERAM DEI [PATRIS] OMNIPOTENTIS (He ascended into heaven and is seated at the right hand of God the Father Almighty.)

In the traditional iconography of the Ascension Christ stands in a frontal position, often held up by

---

*Lorenzo di Pietro, known as Vecchietta,* Articles of the Creed. Christ in Limbo, Resurrection (Descendit ad inferos; tertia die resurrexit a mortuis), *2nd bay, 5th web*

angels. The image is frequently seen engraved in mandorlas. In Domenico di Niccolò's inlays in Palazzo Pubblico which represent the same article of the Creed, the scene does not solely symbolise the Ascension but also Christ seated on the right of his father. The need to remain faithful to the two moments described in the dictate of the Creed influences the iconography used by Vecchietta in the scene. The artist depicts the Redeemer in a perfectly frontal, hieratic position seated on high in the heavens. In traditional iconographic depictions of the Ascension the scene is divided horizontally onto two levels, heaven and earth. On the top level the figure of the Redeemer inscribed in the mandorla constitutes the focal point of the scene whereas on the lower level on earth, the astounded apostles are depicted with their faces turned upwards to heaven as they witness the miraculous event. The desire to separate heaven and earth is also discernible in Vecchietta's fresco. Christ dominates the scene from above in the mandorla while the earth below is evoked by a rarefied atmosphere and lovely landscape which stretches out from the towered city to the mountains until it reaches an enchanting seashore inspired by Sassetta's paintings. The tendency towards abstraction and the almost metaphysical rigour which typifies the pictorial rendition of the articles of the Creed is accentuated by the lack of apostles.

On the left of the web opposite James, Amos (AMOS in the inscription) recites from his prophetic book (9,6) [QUI AE]DIFICA[V]IT I[N COELO] ASC[ENS]ION[EM] S[U]A[M] (he who builds his lofty palace in the heavens). Amos was the first prophet to have his words recorded in a book.

VII. The seventh scene is inscribed on Philip's phylactery (PHILIPPUS in the inscription): INDE VENTURUS EST IUDICARE VIVOS ET MORTUOS (From thence he shall come again to judge the living and the dead). On the other side of the web Joel (IOEL) recites the prophetic creed from his book (4:2): IN VALLE IOSAPHAT IUDICABIT OMNES GENTES (in the Valley Jehoshaphat will judge all the nations). In this scene the representation of Universal Judgement can be recognised, or rather the Second Coming of Christ when the all the living and the dead will be judged. Christ the Judge, who declared during the Last Supper "you may sit on thrones, judging the twelve tribes of Israel" (Luke 22:30), is seated in the middle of a circle of apostles as he reveals his stigmata. The Virgin Mary and St. John the Baptist are on either side of Christ. At the bottom of the scene Archangel Michael is armed with a sword but he is not holding up the scales for weighing souls as dictated by the customary iconography. On his right are the just, waiting to be guided towards Paradise by a heavenly host while on his left are the damned, pushed by the devil towards the jaws of

a livid Leviathan, a sea monster mentioned in the *Book of Job* (41:11) who could "shoot flames and spurt sparks of fire" from its mouth.

VIII. The eighth scene is presented by Bartholomew (BARTHOLOMEUS) who professes the revealed truth CREDO IN SPIRITUM SANCTUM (I believe in the Holy Spirit), as attested by Pseudo-Saint Augustine. The inscription on the cartouche of Haggai is visible on the left of the web (AGGEUS in the inscription). It comes from the book of the prophet (2:5): SPIRITUS MEUS ERIT IN MEDIO VESTRUM (My Spirit remains in your midst).

The dove, a symbol of the Holy Spirit, is depicted in this scene. Immersed in a ray of light it descends onto the host, raised in the pyx on the altar. An elegant red frontal in textured cloth with a decorative pomegranate motif holds the image of a lamb with the standard of the Resurrection in the centre while the figure of Christ covers the foreground. The geometrically positioned paving, the antiquated screen and the half busts of illustrious men separated by elegant pillars all exert a strong fascination on the viewer.

---

*Lorenzo di Pietro, known as Vecchietta,* Articles of the Creed. Universal Judgement (Inde venturus est iudicare vivos et mortuos), *2nd bay, 7th web*

## ■ Articles in the Third Bay

IX. The article *Credo Sanctam Ecclesiam catholicam, Sanctorum communionem* (I believe in the Holy Catholic Church, the communion of Saints) can be seen in the third cross vault. Matthew (s. MATHEUS AP.) invites the viewer to read the inscription on the cartouche with his right hand: SANCTAM ECCLESIAM CHATHOLICHAM SANCTORUM COMUNIONEM (I believe in the Holy Catholic Church, the communion of Saints). On the other side Zephaniah (SOPHONIAS) points towards his phylactery with an inscription taken from his book (2:15) HEC EST CIVITAS GLORIOSA QUE DICITUR EXTRA ME NON EST ALTERA (In all the world there is no city as great as I).

The scene in the web contains some quite complex iconography. In the centre the figure of a pontiff symbolises the Church that stands on St. Peter, laying in the ground. The pope holds out the keys to Peter with his left hand while he baptises a catechumen in the water of a font with his right hand. The image is similar to one by Domenico di Niccolò in Palazzo Pubblico. In the eighteenth inlay of the choir he depicted the Church as a mediator for salvation in its role as distributor of the sacraments. In this case the Church confers grace through the Holy Communion while in St. John's Church the path to salvation is revealed through Baptism. The presence of St. Peter is common to both scenes as he represents the power and authority of the Church. The Saint's position as he lies on the ground where

the pontiff is standing refers to the Gospel of Matthew (16:18): "Now I say to you that you are Peter, and upon this rock I will build my church".

X. Still proceeding in an anticlockwise direction, the tenth web rises above the large lunette at the end of the nave on the right. It is frescoed by Pietro di Francesco degli Oriuoli with *Christ washing the Apostles' feet*. The fresco depicts the revealed truth *Credo remissionem peccatorum* (I believe in the forgiveness of sins) with Simon the Zealot (s. SYMON ZELOTES) holding the phylactery. The cartouche also reads REMISSIONEM PECCATORUM. On the other side Malachi (MALACHIA) recites a passage from his book (2:16) CUM HODIO (SIC!) ABUERIS (SIC!) DIMITTE (If you hate her, let her go).

According to the literary source of reference Pseudo-Saint Augustine, the fresco's iconography consists of an image containing a series of meanings which represent the forgiveness of sins. In the scene a priest lays his right hand on the head of the kneeling penitent in front of him in an act of prayer. The moment captured by the artist is that of the absolution of sins "in the name of the Father, the Son and the Holy Spirit".

---

*Lorenzo di Pietro, known as Vecchietta,* Articles of the Creed. Allegory of the Church (Credo Sanctam Ecclesiam catholicam, Sanctorum communionem), *3rd bay, 9th web*

XI. The Christian Creed also includes bodily resurrection. In the web next to the right-hand wall of St. John's Church, the article *Credo carnis resurrectionem* is depicted. This revealed truth is pronounced by Jude Thaddeus (S. THADEUS): CARNIS RESURECTIONEM (I believe in the resurrection of the body). Zechariah (SACHARIAS) points to his phylactery which contains a passage from his book: SUSCITABO FILIOS TUOS (I will rouse your sons, 9:13)

Four angels above play trumpets to gather together the "elect from the four winds, from one end of the heavens to the other" (Matthew 24:31). The dead take on various forms as they emerge from deep cracks in the earth into an atmosphere of great harmony. The scene is crowded with bodies drawn in a clear, flowing linear style. The resurrected figures have bewildered facial expressions.

XII. The Apostolic Symbol ends with the article *Credo vitam aeternam* pronounced by Matthias (S. MATHIAS). Matthias was accepted among the Twelve apostles as a replacement for Judas Iscariot. His cartouche reads E (*sic!*) VITAM ETERNAM AMEN (I believe in life everlasting, amen). The prophet Obadiah (ABDIAS) on the other hand, pronounces the prophetic Creed from his own book (21): ET ERIT DOMINO REGNUM (And the kingdom will be the Lord's). Thus the cycle finishes with a serene image of Paradise, a garden covered with flowers. The scene is composed of two parts; Christ and the Virgin Mary are depicted above, held up by a cloud of cherubs while angel musicians and a series of saints are depicted below. The saints include St. Bernardine and the four patrons of Siena, Ansanus, Crescentius, Savinus and Victor.

The traditional iconography of images showing the revealed truths in the Baptistery has thus been proven to contain exceptional depth and richness at the same time as being illustrative of the city's cultural identity.

---

*Lorenzo di Pietro, known as Vecchietta,* Articles of the Creed. The confession (Credo remissionem peccatorum), *3rd bay, 10th web*

# Decoration of the Large Lunette on the Left

Benvenuto di Giovanni di Meo del Guasta (1436–c. 1509) frescoed the large lunette on the far wall left of the nave with the *Miracles of St. Anthony of Padua*. The style of the fresco is faithful to that of the artist's master, Vecchietta. The frescoes can be dated to around 1460 as can the cruciform windows put in by the architect Bernardo Rossellino who was in Pienza only at that time. This decorative work was part of the finishing touches to the mortuary chapel which the banker Antonio di Carlo di Nicoluccio received permission to build in 1456 and which he refers to as finished in his will in 1461. The altar piece is described in an inventory from 1478 as having "… images of our Lady and St. Anthony of Padua and St. Bernardine with the predella…" It can be identified as the curved table of Matteo di Giovanni (c. 1428–1495) on which the same subject is depicted. It is signed and

*Benvenuto di Giovanni,* Miracles of St. Anthony of Padua, *detail with the* Miracle of the Mule

*Benvenuto di Giovanni,* Miracles of St. Anthony of Padua

*Matteo di Giovanni,* Madonna and Child with St. Anthony of Padua and St. Bernardine, *Museo dell'Opera*

dated 1460 and now sits in the Museo dell'Opera. This altar piece is considered to be one of the artist's most successful pieces from his early adulthood not least for the inclusion of angels around the marble throne. The way they are slightly foreshortened from below is reminiscent of the angels painted by Piero della Francesca in the *Baptism* of Sansepolcro. As the proprietor of the chapel, Antonio di Carlo di Nicoluccio obviously chose to have the saint who bore his name represented.

I. *The Miracle of the Newborn Child* is depicted in the lunette above: a young mother is accused of conceiving a child out of wedlock. Anthony gave the baby the ability to speak so it could testify as to its mother's innocence.

II. *The Miracle of the Miser's Heart* is on the bottom left: Anthony is called to preach at a miser's funeral service. During the funerary speech the saint cites a passage from the Gospel according to Luke (12:34): "For where your treasure is, there your heart will be also." When family members open the casket afterwards they find his heart beating.

III. *The Miracle of the Mule* is on the bottom right: In Toulouse a man without faith declares that he will only believe in God if he witnesses a miracle. The man leaves his mule without food for a few days then offers him some at the same time as Anthony shows him the Host. The animal then turns towards the host and kneels down in front of it.

The Nazarene altar is under the frescoes next to the figure Christ near the column. A gothic tabernacle by Leopoldo Maccari (1828-1909) and designed by Giuseppe Partini (1842-1895) rises up from the altar; this was one of the results of the restoration project in the Sienese Baptistery which started around 1892. It was one of the last pieces of work to be completed by Partini in his role as architect of the Opera del Duomo because Agenore Socini took over the position a short time later. Socini was responsible, among other projects, for the restoration of the fifteenth-century stoup for holy water (on the right of the entrance) and the design for another stoup (on the left of the entrance) made from scratch by Leopoldo Maccari.

---

*Benvenuto di Giovanni,* Miracles of St. Anthony of Padua, *detail with the* Miracle of the newborn baby

*Lorenzo di Pietro, known as Vecchietta, with Benvenuto di Giovanni,* Way to Calvary

# Frescoes
# in the Apse

Once Vecchietta had finished the frescoes on the vaults he turned his attention to decorating the apse. The artist used a quite complex mixture of techniques for the mural paintings in the Baptistery. He employed the "buon fresco" technique alongside painting with tempera and oil. He also used metallic leaf to obtain vibrant effects of light. On the arch above the apse he painted the *Assumption of the Virgin Crowned by Angels* while on the lower area of the apse he did the *Annunciation*, the *Flagellation of Christ* and the *Way to Calvary*. In the last painting, particularly in the cavalcade detail in the background, historians have recognised the hand of Benvenuto di Giovanni. In 1453 the artist is thought to have worked on the little ocula featuring the *Theological Virtues* and the *Acts of Mercy* on which all men are judged at the end of time. The three gores of the conch were frescoed by Michele di Matteo Lambertini, a painter from Bologna whose works include *Jesus Praying in the Garden*, the *Crucifixion* and the *Lamentation over the Dead Christ*.

The decoration on the apsidal side of the church also includes four full length saints on the anterior face of the corner columns. *Blessed Bernardo Tolomei* and *Blessed Franco da Grotti* are on the left while *Blessed Gioachino Piccolomini* and *Blessed Pietro Petroni* are on the right. The heads of other saints can be seen inside niches around the arch which rises over the altar piece. *St. Francis of Assisi receiving the stigmata* is depicted in the middle of the arch while the patron saints of Siena and the Blessed men from the local area

can be seen on the sides. *St. Ansanus, St. Victor, St. Galganus, Blessed Andrea Gallerani* and *St. Bernardine* are on the right while *St. Savinus, St. Crescentius, Blessed Ambrogio Sansedoni, St. Catherine* and *Blessed Pietro Pettinaio* are on the left.

The *Baptism of Christ* was completed in 1907 by Alessandro Franchi (1838-1914) and it now decorates the main altar; the altar was constructed by Leopoldo Maccari and designed by Agenore Socini. Franchi's *Baptism* is a devotional altar piece which displays strong religious sentiment and it was quite well received by the local press at the time as it did not contain any "modern madness". Before restoration work was carried out at the end of the nineteenth century the altar was in the apse but then it was reconstructed in the Sale delle Statue of the Museo dell'Opera (due to the reorganisation of the exhibition space by Marco Borgogni, it is now behind Duccio's stained glass window). The altar was decorated with the *Altar-piece* by 'i Brescianini' (see p. 140).

*Michele di Matteo Lambertini,* Jesus Praying in the Garden, Crucifixion, Lamentation over the Dead Christ

# Decoration of the Large Lunette on the Right

In 1489 Pietro di Francesco degli Orioli (1458-1496) was paid for the large fresco which decorates the right-hand lunette depicting *The Washing of the Feet*. In this fresco the artist proves he has effectively and resolutely assimilated a knowledge of perspective which originated with Piero della Francesca in the town of Urbino. The forms seem to move with great solemnity in the space between the classically inspired pillars which prop up the central arch. The subject matter is taken from the Gospel according to John (13:1-16):

Now before the Feast of the Passover, when Jesus knew that his hour had come to depart out of this world to the Father, having loved his own who were in the world, he loved them to the end. During supper, when the devil had already put it into the heart of Judas Iscariot, Simon's son, to betray him, Jesus, knowing that the Father had given all things into his hands, and that he had come from God and was going back to God, rose from supper. He laid aside his outer garments, and taking a towel, tied it around his waist. Then he poured water into a basin and began to wash the disciples' feet and to wipe them with the towel that was wrapped around him. He came to Simon Peter, who said to him, Lord, do you wash my feet? Jesus answered him, What I am doing you do not understand now, but afterward you will understand. Peter said to him, You shall never wash my feet. Jesus answered him, If I do not wash you, you have no share with me.

Simon Peter said to him, Lord, not my feet only but also my hands and my head! Jesus said to him, The one who has bathed does not need to wash, except for his feet, but is completely clean. And you are clean, but not every one of you. For he knew who was to betray him; that was why he said, Not all of you are clean. When he had washed their feet and put on his outer garments and resumed his place, he said to them, Do you understand what I have done to you? You call me Teacher and Lord, and you are right, for so I am. If I then, your Lord and Teacher, have washed your feet, you also ought to wash one another's feet. For I have given you an example, that you also should do just as I have done to you. Truly, truly, I say to you, a servant is not greater than his master, nor is a messenger greater than the one who sent him.

On the altar, once again designed by Socini and sculpted by Maccari, there is a triptych with a gold background by Giuseppe Catani Chiti (1866-1945), a follower of the pre-Raphaelite movement. It depicts the *Immaculate Conception between St. Joseph, St. Anne, St. Elizabeth and St. Paul the Apostle*. The work was done in 1896 and has an elaborate neo-gothic frame by the engraver Carlo Bartolozzi (1836-1922). It contains a strong sense of mysticism and a form of symbolism previously unseen in Sienese painting from that era.

*Pietro di Francesco degli Orioli,* The Washing of the Feet

# Baptismal Font

The project for the Baptismal Font was worked on by several Sienese and Florentine artists and is an expression of a period of intense political interaction between Siena and Florence. The purchaser, the 'Operaio del Duomo' (Master mason of the Cathedral) Caterino di Corsino, was known for the considerable political and administrative ability he demonstrated between 1404 and 1420. He entrusted the task of designing a font for the San Giovanni Parish Church to various masters such as Sano di Matteo, Nanni di Jacopo da Lucca and Jacopo di Corso known as Papi da Firenze. In 1416 Lorenzo Ghiberti (1378–1455) was asked by the Opera to take on the position of project manager. In all likelihood the Operaio was advised on his choice of the Florentine artist by the bishop of Siena (1408 to 1426), Antonio Casini. Casini was a well-educated and cultured Prince of the Church who played a key role in the development of Renaissance figurative arts. In front of the font under the panel with the *Baptism of Christ* there is an inscription which reads *Factum tempore spectabilis d(omini) Bartolomei Iohannis Cechi Operari*. These words refer to the last Operaio involved in the work on the Baptismal Font. Caterino's successors were, in actual fact, Turino di Matteo (1420–1423) and Bartolomeo di Giovanni Cecchi (1423–1435). More specifically these two men continued talks with Ghiberti and brought in Donatello among the new contributing artists.

The hexagonally-shaped monument is positioned on a base with two marble steps. Some evangelical passages referring to the rite of Baptism are inscribed under the cornice: S. Matthaeus. EUNTES DOCETE OMNES GENTES, BAPTIZANTES EOS IN NOMINE PATRIS ET FILII ET SPIRITUS SANCTI. S. Marcus. QUI CREDIDERIT ET BAPTIZATUS FUERIT SALVUS ERIT. S. Lucas. VENIT IN OMNEM REGIONEM JORDANIS PRAEDICANS BAPTISMUM POENITENTIAE IN REMISSIONEM PECCATORUM. S. Iohannes. NISI QUIS RENATUS FUERIT EX ACQUA ET SPIRITU SANCTO NON POTEST INTROIRE IN REGNUM DEI. (*St. Matthew*, 28:19: Go therefore and make disciples of all nations, baptizing them in the name of the Father and of the Son and of the Holy Spirit; *St. Mark*, 16:16: Whoever believes and is baptized will be saved, but whoever does not believe will be condemned; *St. Luke*, 3:3: And he went into all the region around the Jordan, proclaiming a baptism of repentance for the forgiveness of sins; *St. John*, 3:5: Jesus answered, Truly, truly, I say to you, unless one is born of water and the Spirit, he cannot enter the kingdom of God).

The six main panels in gilded bronze are divided by statues depicting Virtues. In 1417 the panels of the Font were commissioned in pairs. Two for the Turini family (Turino di Sano and his son Giovanni di Turino), two for Lorenzo Ghiberti and two for Jacopo della Quercia (1371/74–1438). In 1423 the work did not proceed according to plan, one scene was taken away from Jacopo and given to Donatello (c. 1386–1466). The relief panels were consigned in 1427 except for Jacopo's *Annunciation to Zachariah* which the artist completed in 1429. In the meantime Jacopo had been working on other aspects of the Font, sculpting the five prophets in the niches of the marble tabernacle closed in by twin, fluted pillars (which imitate the architectural elements of the funerary monument of Baldassarre Coscia in the Florentine Baptistery by Donatello and Michelozzo). He also worked on the sculpture of John the Baptist on the spire. A cluster of little columns emerges in the centre of the Font and supports the hexagonal tabernacle. The tabernacle is covered with a gored dome on which a pedestal rises up to the statue of the saint. The tabernacle was destined to hold the holy oils of Chrism and Catechumens which were used to baptise people. From the sixteenth century onwards the Eucharist was also kept there.

Lorenzo Ghiberti was the most highly regarded artist working on the project and he received the commission for the statues of the Virtues. However, because of a disagreement over the price two of the sculptures were given to Donatello (*Faith* and *Hope*), three were given to Giovanni di Turino (*Justice, Charity* and *Prudence*) and one was given to the goldsmith Goro di Ser Neroccio (*Fortitude*). Due to the high quality of the last statue it is possible that it was based on a model by Donatello. Above the frame between the triangular frontispieces there were six angel musicians of which three were given to Donatello and three to Giovanni di Turino. They were placed above the external, convex edge and surrounded by elegant shells. At present there are four left. Two by Giovanni di Turino made

in 1431 (looking at the font they are on the viewer's left). The other two, *Dancing Angel* and *Trumpeter Angel*, were done by Donatello in 1429. The third angel by Turino has been lost and the *Tambourine Angel* by Donatello is in the Skulpturensammlung of the Staatliche Museum in Berlin. Another *Dancing Angel* by Donatello, which is quite similar to the putti on the Baptismal Font, is conserved at the Museo del Bargello in Florence. The sculpture shows a certain cursoriness in the finishing associated with the absence of gold and seems unfinished. It is possible that the artist intended to make the statuette for the Font but as he was unsatisfied with the result he put the work to one side and never completed it.

As regards their significance, the

angels could be linked to the *David the Psalmist* sculpted in the niche in front of the entrance. If this were the case, the iconography is similar to the marble inlays of the pavement in Siena Cathedral with the *David* in the centre surrounded by four angel musicians attributed to Domenico di Niccolò dei 'Cori' and Giovanni di Francesco da Imola.

The panel for the tabernacle featuring the *Madonna and Child* was completed in 1434 by Giovanni di Turino. The commission for the panel was originally given to Donatello but surprisingly and regrettably, his work was refused.

---

*Left: Donatello,* Hope
*Donatello,* Dancing Angel
*Giovanni di Turino,* Dancing Angel

## ■ Stories of St. John the Baptist

The *Stories of John the Baptist* are depicted on the panels around the Baptismal Font in a sort of "sculpted biography" according to the Gospels. Here are some of the most significant passages (the passages illustrated on the panels are in italics).

I. The story starts on the panel in front of the altar which was completed by Jacopo della Quercia in 1429 and positioned on the 31st July 1430. The sculpting work on the figures, particularly the one with his back to the viewer in the foreground, shows that the artist drew inspiration from Lorenzo Ghiberti. Jacopo's way of creating spatiality is also reminiscent of Donatello, even though the final perspective effect is different to that of the Florentine artist. This panel is the only proof in existence of Jacopo's ability in the technique of sculpting in bronze. In all likelihood he learnt the art from his father Piero dell'Angelo, who was a goldsmith. The same technique was used by the sculptor to make a panel to obtain the commission for the Florentine Baptistery door in 1401 but the contest was won by Lorenzo Ghiberti and Jacopo's panel was lost. Jacopo's ability, however, lay in the harmony and plasticity of form inspired by the classical tradition in his consistently elegant compositions. The *Annunciation to Zechariah* scene depicts the moment when archangel Gabriel tells the old priest, as he offers incense in the temple, that his sterile wife Elizabeth will soon conceive a son (Luke 1:5–25):

In the time of Herod, king of Judea, there was a priest named Zechariah, who belonged to the priestly division of Abijah; his wife Elizabeth was also a descendant of Aaron. Both of them were upright in the sight of God, observing all the Lord's commandments and regulations blamelessly. But they had no children, because Elizabeth was barren; and they were both well along in years. *Once when Zechariah's division was on duty and he was serving as priest before God, he was chosen by lot, according to the custom of the priesthood, to go into the temple of the Lord and burn incense.* And when the time for the burning of incense came, all the assembled worshipers were praying outside. *Then an angel of the Lord appeared to him, standing at the right side of the altar of incense.* When Zechariah saw him, he was startled and was gripped with fear. But the angel said to him: "Do not be afraid, Zechariah; your prayer has been heard. Your wife Elizabeth will bear you a son, and you are to give him the name John. He will be a joy and delight to you, and many will rejoice because of his birth, for he will be great in the sight of the Lord. He is never to take wine or other fermented drink, and he will be filled with the Holy Spirit even from birth. Many of the people of Israel will he bring back to the Lord their God. And he will go on before the Lord, in the spirit and power of Elijah, to turn the hearts of the fathers to their children and the disobedient to the wisdom of the righteous--to make ready a people prepared for the Lord." Zechariah asked the angel, "How can I be sure of this? I am an old man and my wife is well along in years." The angel answered, "I am Gabriel. I stand in the presence of God, and I have been sent to speak to you and to tell you this good news. And now you will be silent and not able to speak until the day this happens, because you did not believe my words, which will come true at their proper time."

*Meanwhile, the people were waiting for Zechariah and wondering why he stayed so long in the temple.* When he came out, he could not speak to them. They realized he had seen a vision in the temple, for he kept making signs to them but remained unable to speak. When his time of service was completed, he returned home. After this his wife Elizabeth became pregnant and for five months remained in seclusion. "The Lord has done this for me," she said. "In these days he has shown his favour and taken away my disgrace among the people."

II. Two stories for the Baptismal Font were commissioned from Turino di Sano and his son Giovanni di Turino, the *Birth of John the Baptist* and the *Preaching of John the Baptist*. The panels were designed in 1418 and 1420 but they were not consigned until 1427. Turino di Sano was a Sienese goldsmith and had three sons, Barna, Lorenzo and

Giovanni. The oldest son, Barna, was not exactly a sculptor but more of a talented carpenter while the two younger sons were goldsmiths. Giovanni continues to be the most well known member of the family. The reliefs are inspired by designs by Ghiberti and the Sienese artist is known to have developed a close friendship with the Florentine sculptor. In the *Birth of John the Baptist* Elizabeth has given birth to a son while Zechariah can be seen on the left as he writes the name John on a tablet (Luke 1:57–64):

> *When it was time for Elizabeth to have her baby, she gave birth to a son.* Her neighbours and relatives heard that the Lord had shown her great mercy, and they shared her joy. On the eighth day they came to circumcise the child, and they were going to name him after his father Zechariah, but his mother spoke up and said, "No! He is to be called John." They said to her, "There is no one among your relatives who has that name." Then they made signs to his father, to find out what he would like to name the child. *He asked for a writing tablet, and to*

---

*On the following pages:*

*Jacopo della Quercia,* Annunciation to Zechariah of the birth of John the Baptist

*Turino di Sano and Giovanni di Turino,* Birth of John the Baptist

*Giovanni di Turino,* The Preaching of John the Baptist

*Lorenzo Ghiberti,* Baptism of Christ

*everyone's astonishment he wrote, "His name is John."* Immediately his mouth was opened and his tongue was loosed, and he began to speak, praising God.

III. The next scene is the *John the Baptist Preaching. Matthew*'s description of the scene (3:1–12) can be used to understand the panel's iconography:

*In those days John the Baptist came, preaching in the Desert of Judea* and saying, "Repent, for the kingdom of heaven is near." This is he who was spoken of through the prophet Isaiah: "A voice of one calling in the desert, 'Prepare the way for the Lord, make straight paths for him.'" *John's clothes were made of camel's hair,* and he had a leather belt around his waist. His food was locusts and wild honey. *People went out to him from Jerusalem and all Judea and the whole region of the Jordan.* Confessing their sins, they were baptized by him in the Jordan River. But when he saw many of the Pharisees and Sadducees coming to where he was baptizing, he said to them: "You brood of vipers! Who warned you to flee from the coming wrath? Produce fruit in keeping with repentance. And do not think you can say to yourselves, 'We have Abraham as our father.' I tell you that out of these stones God can raise up children for Abraham. The axe is already at the root of the trees, and every tree that does not produce good fruit will be cut down and thrown into the fire. "I baptize you with water for repentance. But after me will come one who is more powerful than I, whose sandals I am not fit to carry. He will baptize you with the Holy Spirit and with fire. His winnowing fork is in his hand, and he will clear his threshing floor, gathering his wheat into the barn and burning up the chaff with unquenchable fire."

IV. The *Baptism of Christ* (1427) was done by Lorenzo Ghiberti who is synonymous with the feat of the Florentine Baptistery's two doors. This panel demonstrates pictorialism and a sense of perspective thanks to the stiacciato relief technique. The linear cadences are very elegant and provide a great decorative effect (they anticipate the stylistic elements of the Doors of Paradise), yet they also demonstrate measured and composed Tuscan Gothic origins. These origins are particularly evident in the sculpting of the Baptist's extended arm, which reaches out to touch the heavenly hosts and the bystanders in the form of an arch and draws attention to the figure of Christ underneath. Even though the episode is mentioned in various Gospels, a passage from *Matthew* can be used to describe the panel (3:13–17):

*Then Jesus came from Galilee to the Jordan to John, to be baptized by him.* John would have prevented him, saying, I need to be baptized by you, and do you come to me? But Jesus an-

---

*Lorenzo Ghiberti,* Capture of John the Baptist

*Donatello,* Herod's Banquet

swered him, Let it be so now, for thus it is fitting for us to fulfil all righteousness. Then he consented. *And when Jesus was baptized, immediately he went up from the water, and behold, the heavens were opened to him, and he saw the Spirit of God descending like a dove and coming to rest on him;* and behold, a voice from heaven said, "This is my beloved Son, with whom I am well pleased."

V. The scene depicting *The Arrest of John the Baptist* is also by Lorenzo Ghiberti (1427). The composition is in the classical style and draws attention to the "humanistic" contours typical of Ghiberti's work. Due to its size the composition has been defined as "towering". The *New Testament* not only explains why John the Baptist was imprisoned, it also reveals the identity of the female figure seated next to a menacing looking Herod. This is how *Matthew* (14:3–5) recounts the episode:

*Now Herod had arrested John and bound him and put him in prison because of Herodias*, his brother Philip's wife, for John had been saying to him: "It is not lawful for you to have her." Herod wanted to kill John, but he was afraid of the people, because they considered him a prophet.

VI. The cycle finishes with the renowned relief by Donatello (1427), *Herod's Banquet*. In terms of its sheer quality and dramatic force, this scene is the most poignant of all the panels. The relief is proof of the considerable results that could be achieved with the stiacciato technique. The great Florentine master is able to give life to the characters in the foreground and still depict other events on different levels, all brought together by spatial organisation. *Mark* (6, 21–29) describes the banquet and the reasons behind Salome's infamous request. Salome is on the right of the relief with her hair tied back:

Finally the opportune time came. *On his birthday Herod gave a banquet for his high officials and military commanders and the leading men of Galilee. When the daughter of Herodias came in and danced, she pleased Herod and his dinner guests.* The king said to the girl, "Ask me for anything you want, and I'll give it to you." And he promised her with an oath, "Whatever you ask I will give you, up to half my kingdom." She went out and said to her mother, "What shall I ask for?", "The head of John the Baptist," she answered. At once the girl hurried in to the king with the request: "I want you to give me right now the head of John the Baptist on a platter." The king was greatly distressed, but because of his oaths and his dinner guests, he did not want to refuse her. So he immediately sent an executioner with orders to bring John's head. *The man went*, beheaded John in the prison, *and brought back his head on a platter. He presented it to the girl, and she gave it to her mother.* On hearing of this, John's disciples came and took his body and laid it in a tomb.

*Andrea and Raffaello Piccinelli, known as 'i Brescianini', Baptism of Christ*

# Works from Other Locations

Various pictorial and sculptural works from the Cathedral and St. Stephen's Church, or rather Santo Stefano alla Lizza, are currently on display in the Baptistery. A saint attributed to the school of Giovanni Pisano (14th century) sits near the left-hand door. Close by there is a painting on canvas of the *Virgin Appearing to St. Philip Neri* (1680) by Giovanni Maria Morandi. This painting was previously on the altar of the Crucifixion in the Cathedral and has now been replaced with a painting of *St. Crescentius* (1863-1868) by Luigi Mussini (1813-1888). Further along there is a stillicidium attributed to the school of Giovanni Pisano (14th century) which depicts a *Lion* and by its side there is a painting of the *Baptism of Christ* by Andrea and Raffaello Piccinelli. These two brothers were also known as 'i Brescianini' after their home town of Brescia and their father, Giovanni Antonio da Brescia, was a dancer and teacher of dance. Andrea del Brescianino worked in Siena between 1506 and 1524 and in Florence in 1525, keeping track of the Florentine painting work of Raphael, Fra Bartolomeo and Andrea del Sarto. The Baptistery's altar-piece can be dated to 1525 and it is one of the most documented of Andrea's works (the other is the *Coronation of the Virgin and Saints* from 1520 which was made for the Augustinian monastery of San Paolo in Siena, currently known as the Oratorio della Contrada della Chiocciola). It is also the only work which Andrea is known

to have collaborated on with his brother, Raffaello del Brescianino (see pp. 100, 125 for information on the altar piece and its original position). A *Saint* from the Sienese school (15th century) and a *St. Michael archangel* from the Sienese school (14th century) can be seen on either side of the Nazarene altar. Near the pillar which marks out the left nave there are two *Angels*. They were sculpted by

(this is the last known work by the artist). The work depicts the *Enthroned Madonna and Child with St. James, St. Stephen, St. John the Baptist and St. Bartholomew.* It is currently on the right-hand wall of the Baptistery. The *Annunciation* can be seen further up and there is a series of *Saints* on the Gothic cornice pillars. The elegant predella by Giovanni di Paolo (actively working between 1417 and 1482) can be traced to the 1440s. The *Crucifixion, St. Jerome,* and *St. Bernardine* are in the centre and stories from the life of St. Stephen are depicted on the sides including *St. Stephen nursed by a deer, The Stoning of St. Stephen, Veneration from the tomb, The Retrieval of bodies of St. Stephen, Gamaliel, Nicodemus and Abibas, Lucian tells the Patriarch John of his vision* and *Gamaliel appearing before Lucian.* Two other canvases from the Church of Santo Stefano can be seen on the counter-façade, *Pietà* by Antonio Buonfiglio (1680–1750) and *Visitation* by Rutilio Manetti (1571–1639). The door which leads to the Sacristy is at the far end of the Baptistery's right-hand wall.

Antonio Manetti between 1831 and 1840 when the artist first became involved with the refurbishment work on the Cathedral of Siena (he also sculpted the great eagle symbolising St. John the Evangelist on the façade of the Cathedral).

The large polyptych by Andrea Vanni (documented between 1353 and 1413) comes from the high altar of the Church of Santo Stefano alla Lizza and can be dated to 1400

---

*Antonio Manetti,* Angel, *right*

*Antonio Manetti,* Angel, *left*